M. FREDERICIC

1987

ZAGAT SAN FRANCISCO RESTAURANT SURVEY

Edited by Anthony Dias Blue
and Edwin J. Schwartz

Published and Distributed by

ZAGAT SURVEY
55 Central Park West
New York, New York 10023
212-362-1313

ACKNOWLEDGMENTS

We would like to extend our thanks to the hundreds of avid restaurant-goers in the Bay Area who were so willing to share their dining experiences with us. Stomach-felt thanks to Marnie McArthur who kept the research project on track, to Mariana Schwartz who kept the restaurant list up-to-date, to Kathy Blue and Bambi Schwartz for allowing the project to overflow our offices on to tables and floors, but especially to our assistant Jack Weiner, who managed to converse with emotional authors (us) and our own "Hal," D Base III Plus, with equal charm and efficiency and still do his good work. We would also like to thank Leroy Meshel for his invaluable assistance.

CONTENTS

INTRODUCTION

Here are the results of our *1987 San Francisco Restaurant Survey* covering 400 restaurants in the Bay Area, including some outstanding places from as far north as the Napa Valley and as far south as Carmel. Nearly 700 people participated in this, our first Survey of what is surely one of the most important and lively restaurant environments in America. Since the participants dined out on an average of 3.9 times per week, this Survey is based on over 2,750 meals per week and 135,000 per year.

Knowing that the quality of this Survey is the direct result of their thoughtful voting and commentary, we sincerely thank each of this year's participants. They include numerous professionals, business executives, members of local food and wine societies, and just plain food-lovers.

We are especially grateful to Anthony Dias Blue, a nationally syndicated food and wine radio commentator and columnist, and Edwin J. Schwartz, a public relations executive specializing in the wine and food field. They devoted much of the past year to helping organize the Survey and to editing the results.

By annually surveying large numbers of local restaurant customers, we think we have achieved a uniquely current and reliable guide. We hope you agree. On the assumption that most people want a "quick fix" on the places at which they are considering eating, we have tried to be concise.

We invite you to be a reviewer in our next San Francisco Survey. To do so, simply send a stamped, self-addressed, business-size envelope to *ZAGAT SURVEY,* 45 West 45th St., New York, NY 10036. Each participant will receive a free copy of the next *Survey* when it is published.

Your comments, suggestions and criticisms of this Survey are also solicited.

New York, New York   Nina and Tim Zagat
May 15, 1987

FOREWORD

San Franciscans' second favorite indoor sport is eating out. There are some 4,500 restaurants in the City and thousands more in the Bay Area. The choice is staggering!

Locals and their guests take their dining very, very seriously. San Francisco's well-deserved reputation as an "open" city, full of free-thinkers and eccentrics, carries over into its restaurants. The eating places of "Baghdad by the Bay" are both diverse and eclectic. In fact, important culinary history was made here.

About fifteen years ago, people in Northern California were waiting around for a big earthquake; they were jolted by a major gastronomic revolution instead. This new California cuisine, pioneered by guru Alice Waters and her Chez Panisse chef Jeremiah Tower, was based on the inventive, unusual use of fresh, local produce. It combined French, Italian, Latin American and Oriental influences into a refreshingly new culinary form. Soon, all over the Bay Area, California cuisine clones began sprouting—offering their own versions of this hip cuisine. Some succeeded in adding new ideas to this exciting culinary style, others corrupted and abused the genre.

At the same time, California wines grown nearby were coming of age. Great strides were made in wine quality and consistency. With its exciting new cuisine and the wines to accompany it, San Francisco and its environs became America's most vital food happening—eats meets West.

Meanwhile, thanks to its diverse mix of ethnic cultures, the Bay Area continues to burgeon with Latin American, Chinese, Thai, Vietnamese, Italian and Japanese restaurants. San Franciscans can legitimately claim to live in one of the best restaurant towns in the country.

San Francisco   Anthony Dias Blue
May 15, 1987   Edwin J. Schwartz

EXPLANATION OF RATINGS AND SYMBOLS

FOOD, DECOR and **SERVICE** are each rated on a scale of 0 to 30 in columns marked **F, D** and **S**:

0-9	=	poor to fair
10-19	=	good to very good
20-25	=	very good to excellent
26-30	=	extraordinary to perfection

The **COST** column, headed by a **C,** reflects the estimated price of a dinner **before** drinks and tip. As a rule of thumb, a lunch will cost 25 percent less.

An **Asterisk (*)** after a restaurant's name means the number of persons who voted on the restaurant is too low to be statistically reliable; **L** for late means the restaurant serves after 11 PM; **S** means it is open on Sunday; **X** means no credit cards are accepted.

By way of **Commentary**, we attempt to summarize the comments of the **Survey** participants. The prefix **U** means comments were uniform; **M** means they were mixed.

The names of the restaurants with the highest overall ratings and greatest popularity are printed in solid capital letters, e.g. "**CAMPTON PLACE**."

If we do not show ratings on a restaurant, it is either an important **newcomer** or a popular **write-in**; however, comments are included and the estimated cost, excluding drinks and tip, is indicated by the following symbols:

I	=	below $15
M	=	$15 to $25
E	=	$25 to $40
VE	=	$40 or above

BAY AREA'S MOST POPULAR RESTAURANTS

Each of our reviewers has been asked to name his or her five favorite restaurants. The 40 restaurants most frequently named, in order of their popularity, are:

1.	Campton Place	21.	Broadway Terrace
2.	Masa's	22.	Zuni Cafe
3.	Stars	23.	Tadich Grill
4.	Donatello	24.	Pacific Hts. Bar/Grill
5.	Chez Panisse	25.	Chez Michel
6.	Square One	26.	L'Escargot
7.	Modesto Lanzone's	27.	Santa Fe Bar/Grill
8.	Cafe at Chez Panisse	28.	French Room
9.	Fog City Diner	29.	Cafe Riggio
10.	Green's	30.	Le St. Tropez
11.	Hayes Street Grill	31.	French Laundry
12.	Auberge du Soleil	32.	Le Castel
13.	Miramonte	33.	Maurice et Charles
14.	Pierre at Meridien	34.	Zola's
15.	Harris' Restaurant	35.	Amelio's
16.	Bay Wolf	36.	Prego
17.	Mustard's Grill	37.	Trader Vic's
18.	Ciao	38.	Le Cyrano
19.	Caffe Sport	39.	Fresh Cream
20.	Sutter 500	40.	Elite Cafe

San Francisco's most popular restaurants reflect the basic eclecticism of the city itself. There are many diverse styles and ethnic types represented, and the places range from expensive and fancy, like Campton Place and Masa's, to casual and moderate, like Cafe at Chez Panisse and Ciao, with all the stops in between. The fluidity of the San Francisco restaurant scene is underscored by the fact that among the top 20, 18 are relative newcomers. There is also a strong representation of "California cuisine" restaurants, which is as it should be in the city that gave this genre its start.

TOP RATINGS AND BEST BUYS

TOP 40 FOOD RATINGS
(In order of rating)

28 – Masa's
Miramonte

26 – Donatello
French Laundry
Fresh Cream
Campton Place
Chez Panisse

25 – Rose et Lafavour's
Mandalay
Le Castel
Bridge Creek Cafe
Cafe at Chez Panisse

24 – Broadway Terrace
L'Escargot
Mustard's Grill
Tung Fong
John Ash & Co.
Swan Oyster Depot
Maurice et Charles
Auberge du Soleil
French Room, The
Rio Grill
Pierre at Meridien
Amelio's
Stars
Osome
Square One

23 – Fleur de Lys
Adriana's
L'Etoile
Ristorante Milano
Hayes Street Grill
La Traviata
Cafe d'Arts
Meadowood
Sutter 500
Plearn Thai Cuisine
Green's
Harris' Restaurant

22 – Bay Wolf

TOP SPOTS BY CUISINE
(In order of rating)

Top American
26 – Campton Place
25 – Bridge Creek Cafe
24 – Broadway Terrace
23 – Harris' Restaurant
22 – Station House Cafe

Top Californians
26 – French Laundry
     Fresh Cream
     Chez Panisse
25 – Cafe at Chez Panisse
24 – Mustard's Grill
     John Ash & Co.
     Rio Grill
     Stars
23 – Hayes Street Grill
     Meadowood
     Cafe d'Arts
–   Butler's

Top Chinese
24 – Tung Fong
22 – Yuet Lee
     China Moon Cafe
     Mandarin, The
21 – China House

Top Continental
24 – French Room, The
22 – Cafe Mozart
     Fournou's Ovens
21 – Doros
20 – Jack's

Top Delis
17 – Max's Opera Cafe
     Acropolis Deli
     Brothers Deli
     Vivande Porta Via

Top French
28 – Masa's
     Miramonte
25 – Rose et Lafavour's
     Le Castel
24 – L'Escargot

Top French Bistros
22 – Cafe Beaujolais
     Le St. Tropez
     Le Cyrano
     Le Domino
21 – Le Central

Top Hotel Dining
26 – Donatello
     Campton Place
24 – Auberge du Soleil
     French Room, The
     Pierre at Meridien

Top Indian
22 – North India
21 – Gaylord
20 – Pasha
19 – India House
     Peacock, The

Top Italian
26 – Donatello
23 – Adriana's
     Ristorante Milano
     La Traviata
22 – La Pergola

Top Japanese
24 – Osome
22 – Kinokawa
21 – Sanppo
–   Kabuto Sushi
–   Ebisu

Top Mexican

21 – La Taqueria
– La Mexicana
– El Tapatio
– Taqueria Tepatitlan
– Juan's Place

Top Newcomers

24 – Square One
Rio Grill
– Butler's
– Circolo
– Dakota Grill & Bar

Top Oyster Bars

24 – Swan Oyster Depot
23 – La Rocca's
21 – Gulf Coast Oyster
Bar Bentley's
19 – Pacific Hts. Bar
& Grill

Top Pizza

22 – Tommaso's
20 – Prego
– Vicolo Pizzeria
– Milano Pizzeria
– Caffe Quadro

Top Seafood

24 – Swan Oyster Depot
23 – Hayes Street Grill
La Rocca's
22 – Tadich Grill
21 – Sam's Grill

Top SE Asian

25 – Mandalay
23 – Plearn Thai
22 – Khan Toke Thai
20 – Siam Cuisine
Cambodia House

Top Steakhouses

23 – Harris' Restaurant
19 – Alfred's
18 – L'Entrecote de Paris
17 – Palm, The

Top Vegetarians

23 – Green's
21 – Vegi Food
20 – Milly's
18 – Diamond Street
– Long Life Vegie
House

TOP 40 OVERALL DECOR
(In order of rating)

28 – Auberge du Soleil
27 – French Room, The
     Campton Place
26 – Donatello
     Masa's
     Carnelian Room
25 – French Laundry
     L'Etoile
     Big Four
     Meadowood
     Mandarin, The
     Madrona Manor
     Modesto Lanzone's
24 – Pierre at Meridien
     Fog City Diner
     Le Club
     Le Castel
     Fournou's Ovens
     Miramonte
     Fleur de Lys

23 – Pasha
     Caprice, The
     Chez Michel
     Alexis
     Blue Fox
     Harris' Restaurant
     Lark Creek Inn, The
     Bridge Creek Cafe
     Gaylord
     Rosalie's
     Bella Vista
22 – Le St. Tropez
     L'Olivier
     Julius' Castle
     Ernie's
     Restaurant 101
     Khan Toke Thai
     Cafe d'Arts
     Fresh Cream
     Horizons

Top Views

Alta Mira Hotel
Butler's
Caprice, The
Carnelian Room
Casa Madrona
Domaine Chandon
Gaylord
Green's
Guaymas
Harbor Village

Horizons
Julius' Castle
Lily's
Mandarin, The
Maxwell's Plum
Meadowood
Pavilion Room
Sam's Anchor Cafe
Victor's
Waterfront

Top Rooms

Alexis
Auberge du Soleil
Big Four
Campton Place
Donatello
Ernie's
Fleur de Lys
Fournou's Ovens
French Room, The
French Laundry

Harris' Restaurant
L'Etoile
Madrona Manor
Masa's
Miramonte
Modesto Lanzone's
Pierre at Meridien
Squire Restaurant
Stars
Trader Vic's

BEST BUYS
Super Buys
(Possible to stuff yourself for $10 or less)

Abalonetti
Acropolis Deli
Adriatic
Angkor Wat
Asia Garden
Aux Delices
Balboa Cafe
Basta Pasta
Billboard Cafe
Bill's Place
Brothers Deli
Cafe Fanny
Cafe Tango
Caffe Quadro
Caffe Roma
Cantina, The
Carlo's Italian
Cheer's Cafe
China Pavilion
Chu Lin
Cuba
Diamond Street
Dock, The
Don Ramon's
Edokko
El Sombrero
El Tapatio
El Tazumal
Ernesto's
Fat Apple's
Faz
Feng Nian
Flynn's Landing
Golden Phoenix
Golden Turtle
Gray Whale
Hahn's Hibachi
Hamburger Mary's
Harbor Village
Hard Rock Cafe
Hunan Restaurant
Hunan Village
Java

Juan's Place
Kim's
King of China
Kirin
La Ginestra
La Mediterranee
La Mexicana
La Rondalla
Les Camelias
La Taqueria
Little Joe's
Long Life Vegie House
Mama's Royal Cafe
Mandalay
Mekong
Mifune
Milly's
Miz Brown's Feed Bag
Nicaragua
North Beach Restaurant
Ocean
Ocean City
Original Joe's
Ramona
San Francisco BBQ
Sanppo
S. Asimakopoulous
Sears Fine Foods
Seoul Garden
South China Cafe
Spuntino
Taiwan Restaurant
Taqueria Mission
Taqueria Tepatitlan
Tien Fu
Ton Kiang
Trio Cafe
Upstart Crow and Co.
U.S. Restaurant
Vegi Food
Vicolo Pizzeria
Vivande Porta Via

BEST BUYS
Good Values
(A bit more expensive, but worth every penny)

Adriana's
A la Carte
Alejandro's Sociedad
Au Relais
Bay Wolf Cafe
Beethoven
Bentley's
Brazen Head
Bridge Creek Cafe
Bruno's
Buca Giovani
Cadillac Bar/Restaurant
Cafe at Chez Panisse
Cafe Beaujolais
Cafe Bistro Oyster Bar
Caffe Venezia
Cambodia House
China Moon Cafe
China Station
Christophe
Ciao Ristorante
Clement St. Bar/Grill
Cordon Bleu Vietnamese
Courtyard, The
Daniel's
Doidge's Kitchen
Ebisu
Eichelbaum & Co. Cafe
Fourth Street Grill
Fresh Cream
Goro's Robato
Green's
Guernica
Gulf Coast
Hayes Street Grill
Ironwood Cafe
Isobune Sushi
John Ash & Co.
Kabuto Sushi
Khan Toke Thai
Kinokawa
Knickerbockers
Korea House
Korean Palace
La Pergola
La Petite Auberge

La Traviata
Le Central
Le Cyrano
L'Escargot
Lucca Ristorante
MacArthur Park
Mai's
Mamounia
Mikado
Mike's Chinese Cuisine
Milano Pizzeria
Mustard's Grill
Nadine
Narai
Narsai's Cafe
Neon Chicken
New San Remo
North India Restaurant
Omnivore
Pacific Hts. Bar & Grill
Perry's
Phnom Penh
Pietro's
Plearn Thai
Post St. Bar & Cafe
Riera's
Rio Grill
Ristorante Fabrizi
Sam's Grill
Samurai
Santa Fe Bar & Grill
Schroeder's
Scoma's
Sharl's
Siam Cuisine
Square One
Stars
Station House Cafe
Swan Oyster Depot
Tadich Grill
Tommaso's
Trattoria Contadina
Vlasta's
Washington Sq. Bar/Grill
Waterfront
Zuni Cafe

ALPHABETICAL
DIRECTORY
OF RESTAURANTS

	F	D	S	C

Abalonetti/S (Monterey) | 14 | 11 | 17 | $14 |
Fisherman's Wharf, 408-373-1851
U—Raffish Monterey Italian overlooking the Bay; it specializes in squid in a variety of hearty preparations; portions are big and service cheerful, but it's generally uneventful—neither food nor decor is earth-shaking.

Acropolis Deli*/S | 17 | 5 | 12 | $7 |
5217 Geary Blvd. (at 16th Ave.), 751-9661
U—A Greek-Russian luncheonette run incongruously by Orientals; expect an inexpensive cross-cultural menu, with stuffed cabbage, sirniki and pot stickers that reviewers sum up as "cheap and filling."

Adriana's (San Rafael) | 23 | 18 | 19 | $15 |
999 Anderson Drive, 454-8000
M—Popular Italian trattoria packed with Marin locals; Chef-owner Adriana Giramonti serves "superb pastas and seafood" in a "homey atmosphere"; anticipate lots of garlic, noise and long lines.

Adriatic*/S | 17 | 17 | 19 | $14 |
1755 Polk Street (at Washington St.), 771-4035
U—Simple, decent, mid-range seafood place that can be an "extremely good value" especially at lunchtime; the decor is pleasant and service is friendly.

A la Carte/S (Berkeley) | 19 | 11 | 18 | $17 |
1453 Dwight Way (at Sacramento St.), 548-2322
M—Creative, homespun American food; some reviewers complain about brusque service and small, cramped tables; recent reports, however, indicate significant improvement.

Alejandro's Sociedad/LS | 19 | 16 | 16 | $15 |
1840 Clement St. (at 19th Ave.), 668-1184
M—Good paella and copious Mexican food attract many to this Richmond district restaurant; the downside of such popularity is crowding, noise and sometimes curt service; there may be long waits, even with reservations.

Alexis/LS | 19 | 23 | 19 | $30 |
1001 California St. (at Mason St.), 885-6400
M—Many like the Continental food at this very fancy Nob Hill spot; others call it "pretentious", "stuffy" and "over the hill"; no one calls it cheap; definitely showing its age.

Alfred's/S
| 19 | 16 | 19 |$20 |

886 Broadway (at Powell St.), 781-7058
*M—Since opening in 1928, the draw at this schmaltzy,
bordello-like North Beach place has been its corn-fed
Eastern steaks; people favor the Italian dishes, but most of
the menu, other than the steaks, is merely "decent"; service
can be inconsistent.*

Alta Mira Hotel/LS (Sausalito)
| 11 | 20 | 14 |$15 |

125 Bulkley Ave., 332-1350
*U—Sausalito tourist restaurant that gets high marks for its
SF Bay views and unanimous pans for its ordinary American
food; service is perfunctory and often downright rude; "great
brunch, except for the food" seems to sum it up.*

AMELIO'S/S
| 24 | 21 | 23 |$34 |

1630 Powell St. (at Union St.), 397-4339
*M – Things have definitely improved here since Chef Jacky
Robert came over from Ernie's; while the great majority
called the French fare "memorable" and "excellent", a few
complain that the nouvelle portions are too small and the
food "just misses".*

Angkor Wat/LS
| – | – | – | I |

4217 Geary Blvd. (at 2nd Ave.), 221-7887
*This new Richmond district Cambodian sibling of the highly
rated Phnom Penh has opened to raves for its fine food and
service; elegant, yet very reasonably priced, it has a charming
floor show to boot; open only for dinner; reservations are
hard to obtain.*

A. Sabella's/S
| 13 | 14 | 14 |$16 |

2766 Taylor St. (at Fisherman's Wharf), 771-6775
*M—Basic Fisherman's Wharf tourist trap that has been
packing them in for over sixty years; mass produced Italian
seafood served by an efficient, old-time staff.*

Asia Garden/S
| 18 | 9 | 11 |$10 |

772 Pacific Ave. (at Stockton St.), 398-5112
*U—At lunch, one of the best dim sum places in San Francisco
and a good value; but our reviewers report the rest of the
menu is standard, unexciting Chinatown food served in a big
barnlike room.*

AUBERGE DU SOLEIL/S
| 24 | 28 | 23 |$35 |

(Rutherford)
180 Rutherford Hill Rd., 707-963-1211
*U—A "little bit of Provence in Napa"; the panoramic view
and snazzy paintings may outshine the mostly Nouvelle
French cuisine that is clever, pretty and pricey; portions can
be skimpy, but few complain since it "feels like France".*

	F	D	S	C

Augusta's/LS (Berkeley) | 17 | 13 | 15 | $15 |

2955 Telegraph Ave. (at Ashby Ave.), 548-3140
*M—Sometimes good, sometimes ordinary seafood that's
served "on Berkeley time—extra slow"; however, sandwiches
and salads on the terrace and tapas in the afternoon get
thumbs up, as do pastas and baked and sauteed fish dishes.*

Au Relais/S (Sonoma) | 21 | 19 | 20 | $20 |

691 Broadway, 707-996-1031
*U—One of Sonoma's mainstays for 15 years offers "good
solid country French food" ranging from "excellent to
pleasant"; a leisurely lunch with a good bottle of wine on the
garden patio will help you forget any culinary shortcomings.*

Aux Delices */S | 16 | 15 | 15 | $11 |

1002 Potrero Ave. (at 22nd St.), 285-3196
*U—Interesting and varied Vietnamese food served in a much
too somber storefront dining room; given its reasonable
prices and unusual food, this Potrero Hill eatery deserves to
be better known.*

Baci/L (Mill Valley) | 14 | 18 | 12 | $19 |

247 Shoreline Highway, 381-2022
*U—Marin yuppie chatter and slick LA decor do not make up
for the second-rate food and "unbearable noise level and
service"; "overpriced, overrated, overstated".*

Balboa Cafe | – | – | – | I |

3199 Fillmore St. (at Greenwich St.), 921-3944
*A trendy singles bar—definitely noisy and crowded—with a
pretty decent kitchen; Jeremiah Tower consulted here and
the menu bears his creative stamp, but the "crowd is more
interesting than the food"; simpler dishes, such as burgers
and salads, are best bets.*

Barbarossa (Redwood City) | 22 | 19 | 21 | $27 |

3003 El Camino Real, 369-2626
*U—"Redwood City's one redeeming feature" and one of the
best Continental dining rooms on the Peninsula, but that may
not be saying much; expensive for the area, and most say
worth it.*

Barnaby's */S (Inverness) | 14 | 16 | 17 | $14 |

12938 Sir Francis Drake Blvd., 669-1114
*U—Beautiful views are frequently marred by disappointing
food and service; stay with the barbecued dishes, ribs
and steaks.*

Basta Pasta/LS |_15_|_13_|_15_|$13_|
1268 Grant Ave. (at Vallejo St.), 434-2248
*M—"The key word here is 'mediocre'"; this touristy North
Beacher has okay decor and passable pasta, but service is
hurried and often inconsiderate; enough people like it so
that lines are long and "Saturday night fever" can be a
real problem.*

Bay Wolf Cafe/S (Oakland) |_22_|_20_|_20_|$19_|
3853 Piedmont Ave. (at 41st St.), 655-6004
*U—Oakland's hotbed of California culinary creativity;
counter-culture decor, a good wine list, large portions of
interesting food and cheerful service draw an enthusiastic
crowd; the menu changes daily.*

Beethoven |_20_|_18_|_19_|$16_|
1701 Powell St. (at Union St.), 391-4488
*U—"Stolid German food"; a North Beach change of pace
that offers hearty cuisine that is a consistent good value in a
charming mittel-European setting with jolly service; bring
your appetite.*

Bella Vista/S (Woodside) |_22_|_23_|_23_|$21_|
13451 Skyline Blvd., 851-1229
*U—Pleasing, Classic French nestled in the Peninsula
redwoods; the view is an important draw, producing a long
wait for window seats, reservations notwithstanding;
charming and courteous service accompany
commendable cuisine.*

Benihana/LS |_16_|_18_|_20_|$15_|
1737 Post St. (at Webster St.), 563-4844
1496 Old Bayshore Hwy., Burlingame, 342-5202
1989 Diamond Blvd., Concord, 827-4220
*U—"Chop chop, chew chew. Next please"; Japanese chefs
cooking and carving your meat at the hibachi tables with
flashing blades is part of the show; it's entertaining, but not
serious; still, your kids will eat it up.*

Bentley's |_21_|_20_|_19_|$18_|
185 Sutter St. (at Kearny St.), 989-6895
*U—A stylish, genteel seafood spot that offers attractive
California cooking and is known for its fresh oysters; though
it's a bit cramped and often noisy, the crowd is attractive and
the food is good.*

Big Four |_18_|_25_|_21_|$25_|
1075 California St. (at Taylor St.), 771-1140
*U—California's rich railroad history is reflected in the decor of
this pricey businessman's luncheon watering hole; classy and
clubby, the American food is "no match for the elegant
atmosphere"; however, some of our reviewers love the
"low-key approach" here and recommend it for drinks.*

Billboard Cafe/LS

| 15 | 15 | 13 | $11 |

299 Ninth St. (at Folsom St.), 558-9500
M—"Far out"; the scene's the thing at this SOMA cafe that serves an eclectic menu to a trendy, terminally hip crowd; the place can be artsy, touristy, or both, with the staff providing a punk fashion show.

Bill's Place/S

| 15 | 9 | 14 | $8 |

2315 Clement St. (at 24th Ave.), 221-5262
M—"Chizburga, chizburga, chizburga" is the refrain at this popular Richmond hangout; though reasonably priced, and though the meat is freshly ground in front of you, this joint is increasingly cited as "overrated" and may be slipping rather quickly.

Blue Fox

| 20 | 23 | 21 | $30 |

659 Merchant St. (off Montgomery St.), 981-1177
M—This "classy" Classic French is renowned mostly for its past, not its present; "elegant" and expensive for sure, but comments about the food, once terrific, now include "tourist trap".

Brad Forrest/LS

| – | – | – | E |

1772 Market St. (near Gough St.), 863-3516
California cuisine with a French twist is what they serve in this comfortable, 13-table boite; it makes for a nice change of pace.

Brazen Head/LSX

| 19 | 18 | 18 | $14 |

3166 Buchanan St. (at Greenwich St.), 921-7600
U—A "great neighborhood place"; the gang watches football here while chowing down on hearty American goodies like chops and burgers; "casual and clubby".

Bridge Creek Cafe/SX (Berkeley)

| 25 | 23 | 21 | $13 |

1549 Shattuck Ave. (at Cedar St.), 548-1775
U—Go for the big American breakfast; homebaked muffins, omelettes, pancakes, fried potatoes and huevos rancheros are all excellent; a recently instituted dinner menu also gets raves; unfortunately, the front of the house isn't as together as the kitchen—long waits are common.

Broadway Terrace Cafe/SX (Oakland)

| 24 | 19 | 22 | $22 |

5891 Broadway Terrace, 652-4442
U—One of Oakland's best kept secrets, this cafe serves innovative, fresh Nouvelle cuisine, but in less than generous portions; its main drawback is its location in a converted gas station; wine only; dinner only.

Brothers Delicatessen/S

| – | – | – | I |

(Burlingame)
1351 Howard Ave., 415-343-2311
*Why is the best Jewish deli in the Bay Area owned by a nice
Chinese couple in Burlingame? don't ask! just eat, bubbie!
have some fruit, too—this is California.*

Bruno's/S

| 16 | 11 | 17 | $12 |

2389 Mission St. (at 20th St.), 824-2258
*U—Massive Southern Italian dishes are to be had in this
traditional Mission district "ol' standby"; "one of a kind";
bring a trencherman's appetite; not much to look at, but
plenty to eat.*

Buca Giovanni/S

| 21 | 18 | 18 | $19 |

800 Greenwich St. (near Mason St.), 776-7766
*U—Good Northern Italian cooking from an "interesting
menu with fine regional dishes"; one of North Beach's better
values—always busy, but serves dinner only.*

Butler's/S (Mill Valley)

| – | – | – | E |

625 Redwood Highway, 383-1900
*Perry Butler (of Perry's) has succeeded in creating a definitive
California restaurant in Marin County; his menu is both
creative and delicious; decor is breezy and modern and
service is so casual, you'd better add up your own check.*

Cadillac Bar & Restaurant/LS

| 17 | 15 | 15 | $13 |

One Holland Court (near Howard St.), 543-8226
*M—"Noisier than a steel mill", this rowdy, loco Mexican
theme park features great margaritas, fajitas and some okay
mesquite grilled dishes; definitely not for the faint at heart, or
those on a schedule; if you're over 40, you'll feel it.*

CAFE AT CHEZ PANISSE/L

| 25 | 20 | 19 | $18 |

(Berkeley)
1517 Shattuck Ave. (near Cedar St.), 548-5049
*M—Popular cafe adjunct to the restaurant that begat
California cuisine ten years ago; it emphasizes freshness and
innovation, but with an Italian accent; while some call the
place "perfection" and "always exciting", others feel it's
"overrated" and "haughty"; the line out front proves that the
former opinions overwhelmingly prevail.*

Cafe Beaujolais/SX (Mendocino)

| 22 | 19 | 21 | $17 |

961 Ukiah St., 707-937-5614
*U—"Good California French bistro"; overlooking the ocean
in Mendocino, this charming country cafe offers one of the
"best breakfasts in Northern California"; Chef-owner
Margaret Fox, a true original, does equally well with lunch
and dinner.*

	F	D	S	C

Cafe Bedford
19 | 19 | 19 | $20

761 Post St. (near Jones St.), 928-8361

U—A small hotel's small restaurant with an exciting, imaginative menu; you get first-rate California cuisine at about half the price of the well-publicized places—a true sleeper; although the room is a "bit dreary", service is professional and pleasant.

Cafe Bistro Oyster Bar */S
19 | 18 | 18 | $16

(Berkeley)

2273 Shattuck Ave. (near Bancroft Ave.), 848-3081

M—Limited French cafe menu in an artsy atmosphere; the bistro-oyster bar combination is an interesting idea which most of our surveyors like; some say it's "ambitious, but not alway successful".

Cafe d'Arts
23 | 22 | 20 | $29

205 Oak St. (near Gough St.), 626-7100

U—"A little gem" that generally gets kudos for its inventive California Nouvelle food and fastidious service; some say "it's too precious and too expensive"; portions are "too small", but we hear few complaints because the menu is remarkably creative and often quite delicious.

Cafe Fanny/SX (Berkeley)
– | – | – | I

1603 San Pablo Ave. (at Cedar St.), 524-5447

Alice Waters' newest creation—a standup finger-food cafe for breakfast and lunch only; small pizzas, dazzling sandwiches and coffee served in bowls are the order of the day; if you don't mind eating on your feet, you'll be pleased by inexpensive food that reflects Alice's remarkable talent.

Cafe Majestic/LS
– | – | – | E

1500 Sutter St. (at Gough St.), 776-6400

Stanley Eichelbaum used to be SF's senior theater critic before he gave it all up to learn cooking and become a restaurateur; this, his second restaurant, serves quite good Californian-American food in an elegantly restored Victorian setting.

Cafe Mozart/L
22 | 21 | 20 | $30

708 Bush St. (at Powell St.), 391-8480

M—A "schmaltzy" and romantic trip to old Vienna with menu to match; although the Continental cuisine is usually praised and the setting called "elegant", there are complaints about service "from Mars" and "funeral parlor" ambiance.

Cafe Riggio/LS
19 | 17 | 17 | $16

4112 Geary Blvd. (at 5th Ave.), 221-2114

M—Hungry mobs pack the bar at this popular Richmond Italian; a no-reservations policy and boisterous crowd pressure the staff and provoke both angry and sympathetic comments; it's noisy and cramped, but offers "the best calamari in town".

Cafe Tango/LS (San Rafael) | – | – | – | I |
1230 4th St., 459-2721
*Grazing food is the current rage and thus tapas, an age-old
Spanish style of food served in little dishes, has come into
vogue; this Marin County tapas specialist does an outstanding
job and is deservedly popular.*

Caffe Quadro | – | – | – | I |
180 Pacific Ave. (at Front St.), 398-1777
*This simple, unadorned adjunct to Square One draws an
attractive, young crowd munching on stylish pizzas and other
Italianate foods.*

Caffe Roma/LS | 13 | 16 | 12 | $10 |
414 Columbus Ave. (at Vallejo St.), 391-8584
*M—Old World North Beach Italian cafe with high ceilings,
frescoes and "great cappucino"; "an easy place to hang out",
it's especially popular for its patio and people-watching; the
service defines "attitude", i.e. usually disinterested,
sometimes to the point of rudeness.*

Caffe Sport/LX | 20 | 15 | 10 | $18 |
574 Green St. (at Columbus Ave.), 981-1251
*M—An assault on the senses; "if you like abuse, this is the
place to go"; but many rave about the Italian food—"best
scampi on the planet", "insulting, but delicious"; despite its
deficiencies, Caffe Sport remains crowded and noisy.*

Caffe Venezia/S (Berkeley) | 19 | 17 | 17 | $14 |
1903 University Ave., 849-4681
*M—"Okay" basic Italian—pasta, garlic and long lines;
sharing tables European-style and live, bombastic opera can
be fun if you're in the mood and come with a group of
like-minded friends; it can also be a royal pain.*

California Cafe Bar & Grill/S | 18 | 17 | 18 | $16 |
900 Bush St. (at Taylor St.), 775-2233
6795 Washington St., Yountville, 707-944-2330
60 Belvedere Dr., Strawberry Village, 381-0800
6090 Redwood Blvd. (Rowland Blvd. exit), 892-0779
*M—California cuisine in a "corporate format"; all locations
seem to be under the same spell: "great menu ideas, but
needs work—food just misses"; to avoid inconsistent results
order carefully and stay on the simple side.*

California Culinary Academy | 19 | 18 | 19 | $20 |
625 Polk St. (at Turk St.), 771-3500
*M—It's the luck of the draw at this attractive cooking school
cum restaurant; the cooks are students and you're their
guinea pig; the students get "A" for effort, but their results,
while usually successful, are uneven.*

	F	D	S	C

Cambodia House
| 20 | 18 | 18 | $14 |

5625 Geary Blvd. (at 20th Ave.), 668-5888
*U—The authentic, spicy Cambodian food at this pleasant
inexpensive Richmond spot has attracted raves and crowds
since it opened; comments such as "exotic food plus
meticulous service" and "amazing combinations of
interesting ingredients" are typical.*

CAMPTON PLACE/S
| 26 | 27 | 25 | $35 |

340 Stockton St. (at Sutter St.), 781-5155
*U—"If you have the money, this is the place"; one of the
brighter stars in the culinary firmament, Chef Bradley Ogden,
revitalizes traditional American dishes with a simple
sophistication and style that win him high marks across the
board; though pricey and though service is occasionally
flawed, this is definitely a star—it ranks first in our Survey for
overall popularity.*

Cantina, The/LS (Mill Valley)
| 14 | 17 | 16 | $10 |

651 East Blithedale Ave., 381-1070
*M—Tex-Mex for the Marin singles crowd; it's cheap, fun,
noisy, and always busy; after long waits downing margaritas,
many are too smashed to even care about the food—
sometimes that's just as well; no reserving.*

Caprice, The/S (Tiburon)
| 18 | 23 | 19 | $23 |

2000 Paradise Dr., 435-3400
*M—Such beautiful views should be licensed only to the
worthy; the view is certainly lovely, but the Classic French
cuisine and perfunctory service here are a real bring-down.*

Caravansary
| 15 | 13 | 14 | $14 |

310 Sutter St. (at Grant Ave.), 362-4640
*U—Middle Eastern snackery offering slightly exotic light
food; convenient and reasonably priced pit stop for
Downtown shoppers.*

Carlo's Restaurant (San Rafael)
| – | – | – | M |

1700 Fourth St., 457-6252
*The "excellent" fresh pasta and great Italian wine list at this
Marin County ristorante redeem an uninteresting setting; it's
a bargain to boot.*

Carnelian Room/S
| 18 | 26 | 21 | $29 |

555 California St. (at Taylor St.), 433-7500
*M—This tourist mecca boasts a spectacular setting atop the
Bank of America building, SF's tallest; but there's trouble
in paradise—the fancy Continental food is somewhat
institutional and service, though competent, is stiff.*

	F	D	S	C

Casa Madrona (Sausalito) | – | – | – | M |
801 Bridgeway St., 331-5888
*Attached to the attractive Casa Madrona Inn, the entire
experience at this Marin County French restaurant is
maximally romantic; a great view of the Bay is matched by
outstanding cuisine and a new chef who promises great
culinary rewards.*

Celadon, The/S | – | – | – | M |
881 Clay St. (at Stockton St.), 982-1168
*Perhaps Chinatown's best fancy restaurant; expect an elegant
setting, formal service and fine Mandarin cooking; a great
place to have crab or lobster.*

Chambord | 17 | 17 | 18 | $20 |
152 Kearny St. (at Sutter St.), 434-3688
*U—"Plain, simple, unpretentious" Continental; a nice place,
with a light and airy atmosphere and pleasant service; good
for business lunches.*

Chantilly/L (Palo Alto) | 23 | 22 | 23 | $26 |
530 Ramona St. (near University Ave.), 321-4080
*U—"Old-fashioned French", but our reviewers like it on all
counts: cuisine—"imaginative", setting—"charming",
service—"great"; it's not cheap, but who cares after the
wonderful souffles.*

Cheer's Cafe/LS | 16 | 15 | 15 | $10 |
127 Clement St. (at 3rd Ave.), 387-6966
*U—"Nice local Richmond cafe" with okay California cuisine;
uneventful, but busy for lunch and brunch; "cute and
modern" and open 'til midnight.*

Chez Michel/LS | 22 | 23 | 21 | $28 |
804 North Point (at Hyde St.), 771-6077
*M—"Tres Francais"; near the Wharf, this "romantic" place
and its fine French kitchen have been charming a loyal
clientele for 15 years; however, our reviewers report that
service and food can be erratic and portions are sometimes
small for the price.*

CHEZ PANISSE/S (Berkeley) | 26 | 21 | 22 | $39 |
1517 Shattuck Ave. (near Cedar St.), 548-5049
*U—Here's where Alice Waters initiated the California cuisine
freshness frenzy 12 years ago; it's nice to report that the
original is still innovative and exciting, outperforming the
legion of its imitators; most of our respondents love the place,
but some complain that the set dinner offers no choice and,
perhaps due to inflated expectations, a few report being
disappointed; reservations are a must; "an experience not to
be missed!"*

27

China House/S | 21 | 17 | 16 |$19 |
501 Balboa Ave. (near 8th Ave.), 386-8858
2237 Powell St. (at Bay St.), 398-8988
U—Mostly of Shanghai derivation, the food here is unusual, tasty and quite refined; prices are higher than in some Chinese bargain joints, but the place is more comfortable and the food delicious.

China Moon Cafe | 22 | 16 | 20 |$23 |
639 Post St. (near Taylor St.), 775-4789
M—Barbara Tropp's new unusual Chinese restaurant has an American eclectic accent; it's "a foodie must" even if "only a few dishes are great"; despite luncheonette decor and uncomfortable booth seating, outstanding appetizers and fanciful main courses deserve to be tried.

China Pavilion */S (Concord) | 14 | 17 | 15 |$12 |
2050 Diamond Blvd., 827-2212
U—None of our reviewers could work up much enthusiasm for this standard East Bay Chinese; the railroad station setting didn't excite many people either.

China Station (Berkeley) | 13 | 16 | 15 |$13 |
700 University St., 548-7880
M—"So-so" East Bay Cantonese; our reviewers find it "nothing to rave about" although some think it's a "good place to take the kids".

Christophe/S (Sausalito) | 20 | 18 | 19 |$20 |
1919 Bridgeway St., 332-9244
U—Charming Sausalito French bistro that offers "excellent rack of lamb"; tiny, but cozy and quite lovely.

Chu Lin */S | 18 | 11 | 11 |$10 |
2428 Clement St. (near 25th Ave.), 668-6266
M—Reviewers rate this nondescript Richmond place a thin chopstick above standard Chinese fare; it takes skill to flush the good dishes out of a predictable menu; those who like it say "try the stuffed chicken wings or the lemon chicken".

Ciao Ristorante/S | 20 | 21 | 18 |$17 |
230 Jackson Ave. (near Battery St.), 982-9500
M—Trendy singles are in full attendance at this stylish Northern Italian spot; though certainly better than most local Italians and though it has a "real feeling of Milan", CR is part of a chain and it shows; some praise the pastas and veal, but service can be slipshod.

	F	D	S	C

Circolo | – | – | – | M |
161 Sutter St. (off Kearny St.), 362-0404
*Brand new and quite attractive Northern Italian that has
moved into the digs of the defunct Old Poodle Dog and
overnight has become a chic spot for a business lunch;
features homemade pasta and stylish pizzas.*

Clement Street Bar & Grill/S | – | – | – | M |
708 Clement St. (near 8th Ave.), 386-2200
*A Richmond district surprise; good, reasonably priced
California fare, including first-rate burgers and inventive
pasta specialties in an attractive setting.*

Cliff House | – | – | – | M |
1090 Point Lobos Ave. (near Great Highway), 386-3330
*Face it, this Continental has the view, but not much more;
look west and you can see Guam; but restaurants with great
views are weak on food, right? right; the ambiance and
service are acceptable, but the cooking isn't.*

Cordon Bleu Vietnamese/S | 18 | 11 | 15 | $14 |
1574 California St. (near Polk St.), 673-5637
771 O'Farrell St. (near Larkin St.), 441-4581
*U—Among the city's first quality Vietnamese places, these
tiny cafes have a strong following; they are consistently
praised for being "cheap and surprisingly good".*

Courtyard, The/S | – | – | – | M |
2436 Clement St. (at 25th Ave.), 386-7616
*A charming American noted for good values in both food
and wine; some nice culinary surprises keep the cafe a local
favorite despite occasional lapses; certainly one of the best
bars in the Richmond.*

Cuba/S | 15 | 6 | 13 | $12 |
2886 16th St. (near South Van Ness Ave.), 864-9871
*M—A greasy spoon offering interesting Cuban dishes such as
seafood zarzuela; some say it's overpriced and "wouldn't last
a day in Miami".*

Dal Baffo (Menlo Park) | 21 | 17 | 22 | $26 |
878 Santa Cruz, 325-1588
*M—Suburban Italian that gets mixed reviews; most feel
it's "expensive, but the food and service are worth it";
others say the "food is not up to expectations" and
is "ordinary".*

29

	F	**D**	**S**	**C**

Dakota Grill and Bar/S — | — | — | — | M
(Berkeley)
2086 Allston Way (at Shattuck Ave.), 841-3848
*Reviewers praise Chef Daniel Malzhan's new Southwest
cuisine as "exciting" and "innovative"; try breakfast, lunch or
dinner in the Southwest-style Shattuck Hotel—an oasis that
has become an overnight success*

Daniel's/S (San Rafael) — 20 | 14 | 16 | $14
1131 4th St., 457-5288
*M—Unpretentious French country cuisine in a cramped little
Marin bistro; reviewers note that it is "very crowded and
small", but they praise the good food and even better prices.*

Da Sandro */S — 15 | 18 | 15 | $13
347 Presidio Ave. (at Sacramento St.), 929-0402
*M—Pleasant, but undistinguished, Pacific Heights Italian
with attractive decor and a nice patio; though "nothing to
rave about", it's convenient to Sacramento Street shopping.*

Diamond Street Restaurant/S — 18 | 14 | 16 | $11
737 Diamond St. (at 24th St.), 285-6988
*U—Hippie eatery that serves reliably good veggies and
seafood—especially the salmon; some think the place is
a bit passe.*

Dixie Cafe/S — 15 | 17 | 16 | $16
532 Columbus Ave. (at Union St.), 397-1509
*U—Cited as a "cookie cutter Cajun", this "yuppie clone of
The Elite Cafe" is panned for "dull food and matching
service", but its warm wood decor and easy North Beach
location keep this bar busy; many consider it lively fun.*

Dock, The/S (Tiburon) — 12 | 17 | 13 | $12
25 Main St., 435-4559
*M—The glorious sun and prime SF Bay views at this Tiburon
Continental are accompanied by "lousy food and iffy
service"; most of our surveyors praise the ambiance and
vilify the food—"should get a chef who can do something
besides hamburgers".*

Doidge's Kitchen */S — 24 | 18 | 22 | $16
2217 Union St. (at Fillmore St.), 921-2149
*U—Basic, unpretentious, all-American breakfasts with
friendly, efficient service; we hear raves over the "good fresh
fruit and home-baked breads" and the "great brunch".*

Domaine Chandon/S (Yountville) | – | – | – | E |
California Drive, 944-2892
Serious French cuisine in a dramatic, modern concrete-construction Napa winery; Philippe Jeanty is a talented chef who can hit the heights when he puts his mind to it; expect breezy service and the sparkling wine to be flowing.

DONATELLO/S | 26 | 26 | 25 |$35 |
501 Post St. (at Mason St.), 441-7182
U—Generally considered the best Italian restaurant in San Francisco, this jewel box of a restaurant offers top flight Northern Italian food; the cooking is very good—with excellent pastas, veal and quail; service is smoothly professional.

Don Ramon's | 15 | 16 | 17 |$12 |
225 11th St. (near Folsom St.), 864-2700
U—Hefty rations of Americanized Mexican munchies in this speedy SOMA spot; great service—"if you're in a rush".

Doros | 21 | 20 | 21 |$29 |
714 Montgomery St. (near Jackson St.), 397-6822
M—Old-style Northern Italian chestnut and a Downtown SF institution for more than 20 years; owner Don Dionda has maintained a solid traditional, if somewhat dated, menu; big red booths comfort a loyal following of the Bay Area's power elite.

Ebisu * | 23 | 17 | 21 |$14 |
1283 9th Ave. (at Irving St.), 566-1770
U—The fine art of sushi preparation gets a charming showcase here; it's the real thing—a solid choice for sushi and all the fixins; attentive service too.

Edokko */S (Berkeley) | 21 | 14 | 13 | $9 |
2215 San Pablo Ave., 841-9505
M—Solid sushi; though generally praised, some say it's "average and unimaginative"; all agree "it's good for the price".

Eichelbaum & Co. Cafe/S | 20 | 13 | 17 |$15 |
2417 California St. (at Fillmore St.), 929-9030
M—Tiny "neighborhood coffee shop" that caters to an upscale Pacific Heights clientele with a great breakfast and lunch menu that is served into the evening; "crowded, casual and good", this Cafe Majestic sibling is not much in the looks department and sometimes exhibits surly service.

El Drisco Hotel/S | 17 | 20 | 19 |$18 |
2901 Pacific Ave. (at Broderick St.), 346-2880
*M—Slightly seedy Pacific Heights hotel with a comfortable
dining room that offers romantic ambiance and unremarkable
California food.*

Elite Cafe, The/LS | 20 | 17 | 17 |$17 |
2049 Fillmore Ave. (near California St.), 346-8668
*M—One of the Bay Area's first Cajun hot spots, this Pacific
Heights deco-style cafe is trendy, noisy and young; some
reviewers doubt its authenticity and value, but the gumbo,
blackened redfish, and jam-packed oyster bar are a big draw.*

El Sombrero/X | 15 | 15 | 15 |$11 |
5800 Geary Blvd. (at 22nd Ave.), 221-2382
*M—Despite liking the "great margaritas and handmade
tortillas [on weekends]" most reviewers call this Richmond
district Mexican "predictable" and find the place "dark
and dingy".*

El Tapatio */S | 20 | 11 | 19 | $9 |
475 Francisco St. (near Bay St.), 981-3018
*U—Fairly popular Fisherman's Wharf Mexican where "the
Chili Colorado is mouthwatering"; some praise it for being
"only somewhat tacky"; service is friendly.*

El Tazumal Restaurant | 19 | 11 | 16 |$10 |
& Taqueria */LS
3522 20th St., 550-0935
*U—A Salvadorean cantina that offers a bargain Latin change
of pace in the Mission district; reviewers praise the "unusual
dishes of high quality" like great tongue, ceviche or the
papusas; they rave about the prices.*

Empress of China/S | 15 | 20 | 17 |$20 |
838 Grant Ave. (near Clay St.), 434-1345
*M—The name gives it away: a Cantonese tourist banquet
hall; it's a nice place, but there is better Chinese food in
Chinatown and elsewhere; the menu is decent, but
mundane; only the view is outstanding.*

Ernesto's */LS | 20 | 14 | 18 |$12 |
2311 Clement St. (near 24th Ave.), 386-1446
*U—Italian dive prized by locals who get in line for the free
garlic bread and glass of wine; the food is genuine, homey
and a good value; some praise the "personable waiters" and
"outrageous chicken dishes"; all mention the low price.*

ERNIE'S/S | 20 | 22 | 21 |$36 |

847 Montgomery St. (near Pacific St.), 397-5969
*M—Old-fashioned "pomp and circumstance" and sometimes
very good; this pricey Continental, with its flocked walls and
1890s bordello decor, is a SF classic, but most say it is now
"resting on past laurels"; still worth a visit.*

Fat Apple's Restaurant | 21 | 13 | 16 |$19 |
and Bakery/SX (El Cerrito)

7525 Fairmont Ave., 528-3433
*U—Often cited as having the best burger in the East Bay, this
popular local joint is also known for its pies and pastries; our
reviewers praise the service and values.*

Faz Restaurant & Bar | – | – | – | I |

132 Bush St. (near Sansome St.), 364-4484
*This narrow building is an historic landmark; it has an
American menu and is also a good place for smoked fish
and game.*

Feng Nian/S (Sausalito) | 18 | 10 | 15 |$12 |

2650 Bridgeway St., 331-5300
*M—"The best Chinese food in Sausalito"; though the setting
and service do not measure up, it's still a very good value.*

Fior d'Italia/S | 17 | 17 | 18 |$20 |

601 Union St. (at Columbus Ave.), 986-1886
*M—One of San Francisco's oldest Italian restaurants, but the
years have taken their toll; reviewers call "this old standby"
"nothing special", "overrated" and "disappointing", but we
also hear that it may be "making an effort to improve".*

FLEUR DE LYS | 23 | 24 | 24 |$40 |

777 Sutter St. (near Jones St.), 673-7779
*U—Expect exquisite haute Nouvelle cuisine created by
Hubert Keller who trained at the three-star Auberge de l'Il in
Alsace; it's a handsome room with professional, deferential
service; sometimes stuffy, always expensive, it can often
be dazzling.*

Flynn's Landing/S (Sausalito) | 13 | 14 | 14 |$13 |

303 Johnson St., 332-0131
*U—Laid-back Sausalito seafood place with lovely views of
the yacht club and modest prices; the decor follows a woody,
nautical theme; everything will be okay if you just stick
to basics.*

FOG CITY DINER/LS | 21 | 24 | 19 |$18 |
1300 Battery St. (at Lombard St.), 982-2000
M—This upscale diner is SF's trendiest, hippest hangout and grazer's paradise; the food, designed by Cindy Pawlcyn of Mustard's fame, can be excellent—insiders recommend the "small plates"; detractors complain about the noise, "offensive waiters" and "the snotty hostess"; in any case this place has to be seen to be believed.

Fournou's Ovens/LS | 22 | 24 | 23 |$31 |
905 California St. (at Powell St.), 989-1910
M—The restaurant of the Stanford Court Hotel on Nob Hill was once considered tops in the city; now it's "slowly becoming ordinary"; it "feels rich and is expensive and the food is good, but not great"; only the wine list and the ambiance are outstanding.

Four Star Restaurant | 16 | 18 | 18 |$19 |
3 Embarcadero Center, 397-4422
M—Lots of "yawns" for this Embarcadero "yuppie hangout"; at best people say it's "good, but not memorable"; try the "squid salad".

FOURTH STREET GRILL/S | 22 | 18 | 19 |$19 |
(Berkeley)
1820 4th St. (at Hearst St.), 849-0526
M—One of the initial group of restaurants that put California cuisine on the map, this popular trend-setter may be teetering; some say it has "gone downhill" and has "pretentious service"; others say this Berkeley institution is on the way back and offers "quality ingredients, excellent preparations and generous portions".

FRENCH LAUNDRY (St. Helena) | 26 | 25 | 25 |$29 |
Washington & Creek Sts., 707-944-2380
M—This mellow wine country place has been packing them in for years thanks to very good French-California food and "the most beautiful bar in America"; it's not always brilliant and the wait between courses can be interminable.

FRENCH ROOM, THE/S | 24 | 27 | 24 |$32 |
495 Geary Blvd. (at Taylor St.), 775-4700
U—The Bay Area's most handsome traditional dining room at the Clift Hotel offers an award-winning wine list, excellent service and an imaginative and beautifully presented menu by Chef Kelly Downs; don't miss roast beef carved from an elegant rolling cart; convenient to theaters.

FRESH CREAM/S (Monterey) | 26 | 22 | 25 |$26 |
100 Pacific St. (at Scott St.), 408-375-9798
U—This prize in the lovely Monterey Peninsula region features consistently clever California dishes served by a friendly young staff; reviewers say "it's still hot" and "best of the good bunch in the Monterey area"; lapses are only occasional; reserve ahead.

Gaylord Indian Restaurant/S | 21 | 23 | 20 |$20|
900 North Point (Ghirardelli Sq.), 771-8822
*M—You get grand Bay views from its Ghirardelli Square
location, but the quality of this North Indian's food is
inconsistent; reviewers tend to hate it or love it; service can be
frustratingly slow, rude or even oblivious.*

Gertie's Chesapeake | – | – | – | M |
Bay Cafe/S (Berkeley)
1919 Addison St. (near Martin Luther King), 841-2722
*The seafood in this popular, noisy East Bay spot is highly
touted, with crunchy crab cakes especially good.*

Gervais (San Jose) | – | – | – | M |
1798 Park Ave., 408-275-8631
*Charming, if "unimaginative", dining room featuring
quality Continental fare at reasonable prices; European
presentations are called "Old World" by some, but the
general view is that this place is first-rate by suburban
standards; "veal and lamb specials are superb".*

Giramonti/S (Mill Valley) | 22 | 18 | 20 |$20|
655 Redwood Hwy., 383-3000
*U— "Homey" Marin County ristorante that's a favorite of
many; the hearty Southern Italian food may be a bit crude,
but our surveyors expect an "excellent dish when Mama
Adriana cooks"; hubby Nino oversees the "attentive service";
p.s. the views are great.*

Giuliano's/S (Carmel) | 21 | 20 | 21 |$25|
Mission Ave. at 5th St., 408-625-5231
*U—One of Carmel's better Italian offerings; the prix fixe
Northern Italian menu is a bargain and the food is inventive
and skillfully prepared; reviewers applaud its consistency and
"attentive service".*

Golden Phoenix */S | 20 | 10 | 14 |$11|
728 Washington St. (near Grant Ave.), 989-4400
*M— "So-so Cantonese that might play in Burlingame, but not
in Chinatown"; like most cheap Chinese places, there are
some nice surprises, like "great oysters on the half shell with
onion sauce"; it's not much to look at.*

Golden Turtle | 20 | 16 | 18 |$12|
2211 Van Ness Ave. (near Broadway), 441-4419
308 Fifth Ave. (near Geary Blvd.), 221-5285
*U—Authentic Vietnamese that has earned very favorable
reviews in a city teeming with Asian competitors— "excellent
cuisine, nice decor, and attentive service"; "Vietnamese at its
best"; charming candlelit atmosphere and reasonable prices;
"try the Imperial Rolls".*

Goro's Robato/S (Mill Valley) | 19 | 20 | 17 | $14 |
591 Redwood Hwy., 381-8400
M—Decidedly mixed reviews on this Japanese—"third-rate" versus "wonderful"; most positive remarks point to the sushi bar as the place to be if you're there, but others say "it's not worth the trip".

Gray Whale */S (Inverness) | 20 | 11 | 14 | $11 |
12781 Sir Francis Drake Blvd., 669-1244
U— "A great place on the Coast to stop for pizza" if you don't mind "laid-back service"; gets generally high marks for other casual dishes and good values.

GREEN'S/S | 23 | 21 | 18 | $17 |
Bldg. A—Fort Mason, 771-6222
M—Old warehouse on the Bay converted to a magical vegetarian restaurant run by the Tassajara Zen Center; "the food is marvelous"; "the waiters are in the ozone"; beautiful location and outstanding views; "the pizzas and pastas are fabulous"; a chic lunch spot so be prepared to wait; "it's become a zoo", but what a zoo!

Guaymas/LS (Tiburon) | – | – | – | M |
5 Main St., 435-6000
Spectrum Corp. (Ciao, MacArthur Park, Prego) came up with this snazzy Marin waterfront place serving "serious Mexican food"; some items, especially appetizers, are first-rate, but the menu generally reads better than it tastes; often noisy and crowded, service can be slow—enjoy the magnificent Bay views while you wait.

Guernica */S (Sausalito) | 21 | 18 | 20 | $16 |
2009 Bridgeway St., 332-1512
U— "French Basque cuisine—as good as it gets"; unusual spice mixtures of Spain and France in a "romantic atmosphere" at very "moderate prices"; most recommend planning ahead and calling for paella.

Gulf Coast Oyster Bar | 21 | 15 | 20 | $16 |
& Seafood Restaurant (Oakland)
736 Washington St. (at 8th St.), 839-6950
U—A swell of Southern cooking is rising in the Bay Area, and this spot is one of the best; despite a "funky location", uninspired decor and some disappointing dishes, people who like the gumbo, oysters, and imported New Orleans sausages say "it's great".

Hahn's Hibachi/S | 15 | 9 | 14 | $11 |
2121 Clement St. (at 20th Ave.), 221-4246
1710 Polk St. (at Sutter St.), 776-1095
M—Korean barbecue cooked at your table; unusual, and often spicy; "great BBQ squid"; it's an inexpensive "simple little place" ideal for experimenting with this unfamiliar cuisine.

Hamburger Mary's
Organic Grill/LS

1582 Folsom St. (at 12th St.), 626-5767
*M—The word "joint" was created for this place; "the decor",
if one abuses the word, is perfectly suited to the funky
SOMA location; "raunchy, but tasty"; most reviewers call it
"fun, but gross".*

Harbor Village

4 Embarcadero Center (at Front St.), 781-8833
*SF's most elegant dim sum offering a remarkable selection of
very refined dumplings and other goodies plus lovely decor
and spectacular views; what more could you ask? Maybe
shorter lines on weekends.*

Hard Rock Cafe/LS

1699 Van Ness Ave. (at Sacramento St.), 885-1699
*M—Hamburgers, chili, salads, milkshakes and mayhem;
"mainly for teens, or would-be teens", this British import is
"exciting if you like loud music and are impressed by rock 'n
roll memorabilia"; apparently the formula works—there's
almost always a wait; we just hope that the Chevy hanging
from the ceiling doesn't fall.*

HARRIS' RESTAURANT/LS

2100 Van Ness Ave. (at Pacific Ave.), 673-1888
*U—Reviewers say "the best prime rib and steaks anywhere"
plus high ceilings, dark wood paneling and attentive service
(jacket required).*

Harry's Bar and
American Grill/LS

500 Van Ness Ave. (at McAllister St.), 864-2779
*Another well-designed Spectrum (Ciao, Prego, Guaymas)
place; the menu is loaded with invitingly authentic Northern
Italian items that, all too often, are botched by the inex-
perienced kitchen; too bad, it was a great idea; let's hope
that another year will whip this place into shape.*

Hayes Street Grill/L

324 Hayes St. (near Franklin St.), 863-5545
*M—Prototypical California grill with great seafood, meats,
salads, and french fries; "it's one of the best fish places in a city
that inexplicably has few good ones"; near the opera and
symphony, service can be wildly erratic, ranging from "good"
to "inattentive, almost rude".*

Horizons/LS (Sausalito)

558 Bridgeway St., 331-3232
*U—Seafood house; "go for the view and order something
that can't be burned too badly"; or skip the food and enjoy
the Bay view over a beer.*

	F	D	S	C

Hunan Restaurant | – | – | – | I |

924 Sansome St. (near Broadway), 956-7727
853 Kearny St. (near Jackson St.), 788-2234
5723 Geary Blvd. (at 21st Ave.), 221-3388
*Spicy Chinatown spot that some rate "best in the west"; our
reviewers like the hot cuisine, if not the "garage-like" setting;
go in large groups; bring the Pepto-Bismol; a bargain.*

Hunan Village/S | 17 | 11 | 13 | $11 |

839 Kearny St. (at Jackson St.), 956-7868
*M— "Hunan cooking shouldn't be dull", neither should the
service or the decor, but that's the last word on this Chinatown
spot that is riding on its reputation and its bargain pricing.*

Il Pirata * | 14 | 9 | 16 | $14 |

2007 16th St. (at Portero Ave.), 626-1845
*M— The above ratings reflect shabby decor and ordinary
Italian food, but they do not reveal the positive comments
made by regulars—"nice old-fashioned joint", "great
family-style dining".*

Imperial Palace/LS | 19 | 21 | 21 | $23 |

919 Grant Ave. (near Washington St.), 982-4440
*M— Chinatown old-timer with "beautiful decor and excellent
service, but the Cantonese food can vary"; reviewers say it's
elegant, but too expensive for what it is.*

India House | 19 | 19 | 18 | $18 |

350 Jackson St. (at Battery St.), 392-0744
*M— Dark, dark, dark—romantic, or is it a ploy to hide the
food; once was the Bay Area's best Indian place, but now
others are way ahead of it; still, some reviewers find the food
acceptable and like the atmosphere.*

India Place (Mill Valley) | 18 | 13 | 17 | $16 |

707 Redwood Hwy., 388-3350
1888 Solano Ave., Berkeley, 525-1122
*M— Wildly inconsistent comments about both the food and
service at this Indian—"the Maitre d' was great, but not the
food" versus "remarkably good".*

Ino Sushi * | 21 | 15 | 13 | $18 |

1620 Webster St. (at Post St.), 922-3121
*U—Highly rated sushi bar, "tiny and dependable", and
"family-like" with "Mama-san one of the best waitresses".*

	F	D	S	C

Iron Horse, The/S | 16 | 14 | 16 | $18 |
19 Maiden Lane (off Union Sq.), 362-8133
M—Traditional old-time SF restaurant; "for businessmen and downtown shoppers"; often crowded and noisy and always dark; seafood and veal are their fortes.

Ironwood Cafe | 19 | 18 | 19 | $16 |
901 Cole St. (at Carl St.), 664-0224
U—This "good neighborhood cafe" produces unpretentious California cuisine in a casual atmosphere; it's got "the homeliness of a Midwestern eatery with touches of SF sophistication" and "flair"; desserts draw raves.

Isobune Sushi | 19 | 17 | 17 | $15 |
1737 Post St. (near Webster St.), 563-1030
U—Sushi on board—tiny boats circle in front of diners seated at the large oval bar; pick your own; "gimmicky and good", "a lot of fun".

Ivy's/S | – | – | – | M |
398 Hayes St. (near Gough St.), 626-3930
Under new management, this popular Continental is trying hard to keep up with upscale local competition; its Downtown location keeps it busy during Civic Center events; though unexciting, it does a credible job.

Jack's/SX | 20 | 15 | 17 | $22 |
615 Sacramento St. (near Montgomery St.), 986-9854
M—Uh-oh, another SF tradition bites the dust; living on reputation only, and with "Continental food as stale as the waiters", our reviewers say "this place needs a clean sweep"; it appears only regulars love Jack's.

Jackson Fillmore Trattoria/S | 19 | 13 | 16 | $17 |
2506 Fillmore St. (at Jackson St.), 346-5288
M—New "in-place" for large family-style portions of Southern Italian food; it has become a cult hangout overnight and is now stressed with long waits, crowding and perfunctory service; given its nonexistent decor and greasy, crudely prepared cuisine, it's hard to understand what the fuss is all about.

Java Restaurant/LS | 19 | 12 | 19 | $10 |
417 Clement St. (near 5th Ave.), 752-1541
U—Small Richmond area Indonesian offers unusual items that are "cheap and good"; try the coconut sauced dishes or the spicy french fries (they're "to cry over").

F	D	S	C

Jil's Trianon
| – | – | – | E |

(f/k/a Rene Verdon's Le Trianon)
242 O'Farrell St. (near Powell St.), 982-9353
This Classic French citadel was recently sold to Dutch
restaurateurs who have redecorated and put in a new
American-Continental menu; could be a Dutch treat—time
will tell.

JOHN ASH & CO. /S
| 24 | 19 | 22 | $22 |

(Santa Rosa)
2324 Montgomery Drive, 707-527-7687
U—Innovative California cuisine serving food lovingly
prepared from the finest produce with one of "the best wine
lists in California"; this has got to be high on any list of wine
country restaurants.

Juan's Place (Berkeley)
| – | – | – | I |

941 Carleton St., 845-6904
Why such crowds in this East Bay Mex spot? How about good
food, good service, fair prices and FRESH tortilla chips.

Julius' Castle /S
| 15 | 22 | 16 | $28 |

1541 Montgomery St. (at Union St.), 362-3042
M—The view from the top of Telegraph Hill makes a popular
tourist attraction, but a boring Continental menu served with
"condescending arrogance" causes most reviewers to scale
other heights.

Kabuto Sushi /LS
| 24 | 18 | 20 | $17 |

5116 Geary Blvd. (at 15th Ave.), 752-5652
U—Unquestionably the "best sushi in town"; this is the real
stuff—fresh, exotic and delicious; add pleasant ambiance and
beautiful presentation, all at reasonable prices, and you'll
understand why KS gets consistent raves; open until 2 AM.

Kan's /S
| 18 | 18 | 19 | $19 |

708 Grant Ave. (near Sacramento St.), 982-2388
M—Once proud Chinatown palace that some say serves the
"most ordinary Cantonese food ever encountered"; except
for still popular duck dishes, most diners find the food
is undistinguished.

Kansai *
| 20 | 18 | 18 | $16 |

325 Sacramento St. (near Battery St.), 392-2648
M—Attractive Embarcadero Japanese that draws mixed
notices; some praise the sushi and the Kyoto-style
meals; others say this simple, modern place has gone
drastically downhill.

Khan Toke Thai House/S | 22 | 22 | 20 |$15 |
5937 Geary Blvd. (at 24th Ave.), 668-6654
U—Popular Richmond area Thai where you check your shoes and sit on the floor; it's "fun when you get into the mood"; the extensive menu is rich, spicy and delicious, decor is darkly romantic, and service attentive; definitely not for the oldsters or anyone with a bad back—"a chiropractor could make a good living next door".

Kim's/S | – | – | – | I |
508 Presidio Ave. (at California St.), 923-1500
Charming Vietnamese-Continental in Presidio Heights; small, cozy and surprisingly elegant; refined Viet dishes and lovely grilled fish and meat; charming service; don't miss the catfish.

King of China | – | – | – | I |
939 Clement St. (off 11th Ave.), 668-2618
Chinese banquet hall the size of an airplane hangar with mirrors to boot; intimate it ain't, but the dim sum downstairs and grand Chinese banquets upstairs make it worth a try.

Kinokawa/LS | 22 | 15 | 20 |$16 |
347 Grant Ave. (near Bush St.), 956-6085
M—Downtown Japanese with sushi that draws high marks as well as a full menu of cooked foods; though convenient for shoppers, some dislike the "dark and claustrophobic" ambiance.

Kirin*/S | 19 | 8 | 14 |$12 |
6135 Geary Blvd. (near 25th Ave.), 752-2412
M—Richmond area Northern Chinese that has a steady following; best dishes aren't on the menu, e.g., cherry pork and handmade noodles; despite formica decor, this is not the world's most sanitary restaurant, but, at Kirin's low prices, its fans gladly overlook such flaws.

Knickerbockers/S (St. Helena) | – | – | – | M |
3010 St. Helena Highway North, 707-963-9300
"New Age roadhouse" that offers skillful California and Continental fare; setting is breezy and comfortable with lovely gardens and easygoing service; open kitchen and fireplace.

Korea House*/LS | 20 | 13 | 17 |$15 |
1640 Post St. (at Laguna St.), 563-1308
U—Good Korean food in Japantown; "decor needs work", but most reviewers like the spicy food; open until 3 AM.

	F	D	S	C

Korean Palace */L | 20 | 21 | 21 | $18 |
631 O'Farrell St. (near Hyde St.), 771-5353
*U—Formal Korean in a sedate Downtown setting; reviewers
are most impressed with the delicate, sculptural
presentations; traditional and serene.*

Kuleto's/LS | – | – | – | M |
221 Powell St. (off Geary Blvd.), 397-7720
*Stylish, new Northern Italian in Villa Florence Hotel; too early
to judge, but initial reports are positive.*

La Fuente/L | 13 | 15 | 15 | $13 |
2 Embarcadero Center (at Front St.), 982-3363
*U—Downtown Mexican that's best for after-work drinks; our
reviewers pan the "blandest Mexican food in town"; "great
margaritas, horrible food".*

La Ginestra/LSX (Mill Valley) | 19 | 11 | 17 | $13 |
127 Throckmorton Ave. (at Miller St.), 388-0224
*M—"Funky, but authentic" Marin Italian; it's a good place
to take the family; decent food and friendly service at
affordable prices.*

Lalime's (Albany) | – | – | – | M |
1410 Solano Ave., 527-9838
*Tiny East Bay French provincial; the menu changes
frequently and prices are pleasingly low; live music on
Fridays and Saturdays.*

La Mediterranee/S | – | – | – | I |
2210 Fillmore St. (at Sacramento St.), 921-2956
288 Noe St. (at 24th St.), 431-7210
2936 College Ave., Berkeley, 540-7773
857 Fourth St., San Rafael, 258-9123
*Sunny, Middle Eastern cafes offering diners inexpensive food
plus friendly, efficient service.*

La Mere Duquesne/S | 17 | 21 | 18 | $22 |
550 Geary Blvd. (near Taylor St.), 776-7600
*M—French country cooking classed as ordinary and "tired";
attractive decor and reliable service still make it a good
theater district choice; moderate prices.*

La Mexicana */S (Oakland) | 22 | 6 | 18 | $11 |
3930 E. 14th St. (at 40th St.), 436-8388
*U—Popular Mexican food and service in a no-nonsense
Downtown storefront; with the "best handmade corn tortillas
in the world", it's cheap and fun, perfect for taking the family,
"but also a dump".*

La Pergola Ristorante | 22 | 19 | 20 | $21 |
2060 Chestnut St. (at Gough St.), 563-4500
*U—Aficionados beg "keep this one a secret, please";
romantic, small Marina area Northern Italian that draws wide
praise; reviewers point to the "best veal chop outside of
Firenze" and the "heavenly tortellini".*

La Petite Auberge (San Rafael) | 19 | 19 | 20 | $18 |
704 4th St., 459-9982
*M—Popular, attractive suburban place that offers "a little bit
of France in Marin with terrific souffles"; our surveyors praise
the elegant, country atmosphere, but some warn that it has
"grown old".*

Lark Creek Inn, The /S (Larkspur) | 17 | 23 | 19 | $17 |
234 Margolia Ave., 924-7766
*M—Reviewers rave about the "idyllic country setting" of this
Marin County oasis; the Continental menu garners less
praise—"well-prepared"; great brunch spot.*

La Rocca's Oyster Bar /S | 23 | 14 | 18 | $15 |
3519 California St. (in Laurel Village), 282-7780
*M—Swan Oyster Depot clone whose seafood is fresh, but not
quite as high quality as it might be; its Pacific Heights
neighbors find it convenient when they are too lazy to drive
Downtown for the real thing.*

La Rondalla /SX | 13 | 14 | 14 | $10 |
901 Valencia St. (near 20th St.), 647-7474
*M—Mission Mexican that is "living on legend only";
reviewers like the kitschy year 'round Christmas decor,
but say that "Taco Bell serves better Mexican food".*

Las Camelias * (San Rafael) | 20 | 15 | 16 | $10 |
912 Lincoln Ave. (near 3rd Ave.), 453-5850
*M—Marin Mexican that gains lukewarm praise from
reviewers; some like the shrimps and enchiladas, but others
say "overrated"; most agree it gives "good value".*

Las Mananitas/L | 15 | 19 | 16 | $17 |
850 Montgomery St. (at Pacific St.), 434-2088
*M—Downtown Mexican in an elegant, but mildly
claustrophobic cellar location; some people complain of
"microwave Mexican" food, but its specials are worth a try.*

La Taqueria | 21 | 7 | 13 | $6 |
2889 Mission St. (near 24th St.), 285-7117
*M—Mission area Mexican that garners kudos for its
blockbuster burritos and great fruit drinks; its tacky,
"dreadful" decor gets universal pans.*

La Traviata/LS | 23 | 20 | 20 | $17 |
2854 Mission St. (near 24th St.), 282-0500
*U— "Veal and Verdi—Scallopini and Scarpia—what a
combination!"; this Italian opera hangout wins raves for its
pastas and veal dishes; though its booths can be cramped,
this trattoria's homey setting, as well as its arias, make it a hit.*

L'Auberge * (Redwood City) | 16 | 18 | 18 | $21 |
2826 El Camino Real (near 5th Ave.), 365-3735
*M—Comfortable Peninsula French-Continental that's in a
"long slow decline from excellence 15 years ago"; you'll get
classic cuisine at a price you'll remember.*

Le Camembert/S (Mill Valley) | 16 | 20 | 17 | $18 |
200 Shoreline Hwy., 383-8000
*M—Faded French Classic that, despite pleasant atmosphere,
draws yawns—"best microwaved food in Marin".*

Le Candide | 19 | 17 | 17 | $20 |
301 Kearny St. (at Bush St.), 981-2213
*U—Downtown French bistro that specializes in semi-power
lunches that can be "frenzied" and "very noisy"; "the food's
not bad"; especially try the "poulet avec pomme frites."*

LE CASTEL | 25 | 24 | 24 | $36 |
3235 Sacramento St. (at Presidio Ave.), 921-7115
*M—Pricey, romantic Pacific Heights haute French; small and
refined with skillfully prepared food and deferential service;
its cuisine draws superlatives, but there are some who say it's
"overrated" and "too expensive".*

	F	D	S	C

Le Central
| 21 | 17 | 17 | $21 |

453 Bush St. (near Kearny St.), 391-2233
U—Closest thing to Paris in San Francisco; popularized by columnist Herb Caen, this is a real bistro with good, hearty, simple French food; it can be noisy and crowded, but that's all part of the authentic ambiance; a power spot.

Le Club
| 20 | 24 | 24 | $38 |

1250 Jones St. (at Clay St.), 771-5400
M—Nob Hill grand luxe; some like this swanky place, but most call it an "overdone, stilted idea of grand dining"; "overstuffed and overpriced", this French traditionalist with its heavy French sauces and pretentious service is a throwback to the 1950s.

Le Cyrano/LX
| 22 | 19 | 21 | $18 |

4134 Geary Blvd. (at 6th Ave.), 387-1090
U—Small Richmond neighborhood bistro with "good tried-and-true French entrees"; reliable and moderately priced, it's a favorite for its rack of lamb and cheerful service.

Le Domino
| 22 | 19 | 22 | $21 |

2742 17th St. (at Florida St.), 626-3095
M—Haute French near the Galleria Design Center on the wrong side of the tracks; its food gets halfhearted praise; as for decor, it "tries to be elegant, but turns out tacky".

Le Marquis */S (Lafayette)
| 20 | 14 | 19 | $26 |

3524B Mt. Diablo Blvd. (at 1st St.), 284-4422
U—East Bay haute French in a shopping center; the food is consistent, not flashy; newly decorated in muted tones, it's simple and comfortable.

Le Metropole/LS (Berkeley)
| 18 | 17 | 17 | $19 |

2271 Shattuck Ave. (near Bancroft Ave.), 848-3080
M—Country French with a "Berkeleyish" atmosphere; the food hits "some outstanding highs, but also some misses"; however, its calm ambiance is good for conversation.

L'Entrecote de Paris/LS
| 19 | 16 | 17 | $20 |

2032 Union St. (near Webster St.), 931-5006
M—Bistro French that is "spotty—sometimes excellent, sometimes not even good"; desserts and the patio get the biggest applause.

	F	D	S	C

Le Papillon * (San Jose) | 19 | 14 | 17 | $20 |
410 Saratoga Ave. (at Kiely Blvd.), 408-296-3730
M—Peninsula haute French that is "the best in San Jose, but that's not saying much"; overdone pseudo-French decor; passable service.

Le Piano Zinc/LS | – | – | – | E |
708 14th St. (at Market St.), 431-5266
A new star in town; this Castro district French boite offers inventive food and a chanteuse on weekends; it's chic, elegant and not outrageously priced; but service can be haughty and the owner rude.

Le Rhone */SX (St. Helena) | 22 | 20 | 21 | $38 |
1234 Main St. (at Hunt Ave.), 707-963-0240
U—This petite, attractive wine country bistro serves the hearty provincial fare of its owner's Rhone region heritage; although not brilliant, its cuisine is definitely well above typical suburban French restaurants; so are its prices.

L'Escale *(Palo Alto) | 18 | 19 | 16 | $25 |
5 Stanford Shopping Ctr. (near El Camino Real), 326-9857
M—Simple French bistro in a big shopping center; reviewers find the food adequate and the decor pleasant.

L'Escargot/LS | 24 | 21 | 23 | $20 |
1809 Union St. (near Octavia St.), 567-0222
U—Quaint, low-key French that never disappoints; service is "warm yet professional"; it's among SF's better Gallic places for good quality and consistency.

Le St. Tropez | 22 | 22 | 21 | $27 |
126 Clement St. (near 2nd Ave.), 387-0408
M—Richmond French that may be "too expensive for simply a pleasant experience"; a neighborhood bistro with charming ambiance and good food, people take exception only to the price.

L'ETOILE | 23 | 25 | 24 | $39 |
1075 California St. (at Powell St.), 771-1529
U—Grand and beautiful Nob Hill patrician offering reliably well-prepared haute cuisine; the beautiful people are here, clucked over by a professional and skilled staff; the glitterati hang out at the piano bar.

	F	**D**	**S**	**C**

Lily's of San Francisco/L | – | – | – | M |
4 Embarcadero Center, 398-3434
Good-looking, modern Downtown cafe with a formal
weekend dining room; serving American Nouvelle food,
it's pleasant, pretty and popular.

Little Italy/LS | 19 | 12 | 15 | $14 |
4109 24th St. (at Castro St.), 821-1515
"Average Italian served by unfriendly people"; crowded and
noisy; the food is heavy and crude; reminds New Yorkers of
Grotta Azzurra.

Little Joe's | 18 | 12 | 15 | $12 |
523 Broadway (at Grant Ave.), 433-4343
715 Harrison St. (near Third St.), 546-9151
1358 Ninth Ave. (near Irving St.), 759-8090
U— "Great for what it is"—i.e. a "messy but good" Italian
luncheonette that also serves dinners and is always busy; "sit
at the counter and bring your appetite"; lots of fun and the
price is right..

L'Olivier | 21 | 22 | 21 | $24 |
465 Davis St. (at Jackson St.), 981-7824
U— Traditional country French at the Embarcadero that
draws generally favorable comments; it's got a comfortable
setting and fair prices.

London Wine Bar, The | – | – | – | I |
415 Sansome St. (near Sacramento St.), 788-4811
This upscale, wood-paneled wine bar features 20 wines by
the glass and 20 ports and sherries, but serves only a light,
California-style lunch; a must for California wine aficionados
and casuals alike.

Long Life Vegie House/S | – | – | – | I |
(Berkeley)
2129 University Ave. (near Shattuck Ave.), 854-6072
East Bay Chinese vegetarian; hippie-dippie, but the food is
decent; decor gets low marks, but the price is also low.

Lucca Ristorante/S (Mill Valley) | 18 | 15 | 18 | $14 |
24 Sunnyside Ave., 388-4467
U— Modest Northern Italian that draws praise for food, prices
and friendly service; "Monday lobster special is great".

47

F	D	S	C

MacArthur Park/LS · 18 | 19 | 17 |$17
607 Front St. (at Davis St.), 398-5700
27 University Ave., Palo Alto, 321-9990
U—Trendy, yuppie hangout with breezy service; the best BBQ ribs in SF and American food that is consistently praised; a popular place to meet and greet; it's always bustling and usually fun.

Madrona Manor/S (Healdsburg) · 23 | 25 | 20 |$24
1001 West Side Rd., 707-433-4231
U—Fresh and inventive California cuisine in a charming, rustic wine-country house; "a gem! stay overnight"; the staff is young and friendly.

Mai's/S · 20 | 11 | 15 |$11
316 Clement St. (at 5th Ave.), 221-3046
1360 Ninth Ave. (near Judah St.), 753-6863
1838 Union St. (near Laguna St.), 921-2861
M— "Reliable, but unexceptional" Vietnamese; despite a "sameness in many dishes", brisk service and modest prices keep all three locations going strong.

Mama's/LS · 14 | 15 | 14 |$13
398 Geary Blvd. (at Stockton St.), 433-0113
1701 Stockton St. (near Filbert St.), 362-6421
379 Stanford Shopping Ctr., Palo Alto, 327-4735
U—Basic American fare; breakfast draws raves, but take a pass on the rest; a glorified coffee shop that operates like a California restaurant of the 1950s.

Mama's Royal Cafe/SX (Oakland) · 17 | 10 | 15 |$10
4012 Broadway (near MacArthur Ave.), 547-7600
U— "Best home fries around, but is the dingy atmosphere worth it?; reviewers like the breakfasts here, but not much else; the decor is simply grubby.

Mamounia/S · 20 | 22 | 20 |$19
4411 Balboa St. (at 45th Ave.), 752-6566
U—Culinary theater; you sit on the floor on big stuffed cushions under paisley-printed tents and eat delicious Moroccan food with your fingers (no utensils allowed); "honey lamb with almonds is orgasmic"; most repeated comment— "it's an experience".

Mandalay/S · 25 | 14 | 21 |$12
4344 California St. (at 6th Ave.), 386-3895
U—Our reviewers are crazy about this new bargain-priced Richmond district Burmese, e.g. "wonderful food, excellent service, truly a find"; except for the decor, which is merely pleasant, this is an "undiscovered gem".

Mandarin House/S (San Rafael) | 20 | 14 | 19 | $14 |
817 Francisco Blvd. West, 492-1638
*U—Marin Chinese that gets high marks for food and low ones
for decor; "one goes only for the quality of the food",
otherwise it has a "drafty, strange location" and long waits.*

MANDARIN, THE/S | 22 | 25 | 21 | $25 |
900 North Point St. (at Ghirardelli Sq.), 673-8812
*M—Plush, pricey Ghirardelli Square Chinese with great Bay
views; tourists gobble it up, but locals warn "stick with the
specialties, stray at your own peril"; the kitchen is capable of
magic, but you have to push the right buttons and pray.*

Marin Joe's/S (Corte Madera) | 17 | 10 | 16 | $13 |
1585 Casa Buena Dr., 924-2081
*M—Raffish Southern Italian diner with robust, uncomplicated
food; better than Denny's and a good pit stop when Highway
101 backs up; "cheap, lots of food, but the quality is suspect".*

MASA'S | 28 | 26 | 26 | $45 |
648 Bush St. (near Powell St.), 989-7154
*U—Highest-rated for food in the Survey and quite deserving
of the distinction, Masa's is a remarkable restaurant that
works at every level: the French food is exquisitely crafted by
Chef Julian Serrano, service is attentive and intelligent, and
the wine list is excellent; with high prices and rich food, this is
not an everyday place, but it's the special-est of SF's special
occasion restaurants.*

Maurice et Charles/L | 24 | 18 | 24 | $28 |
(San Rafael)
901 Lincoln Ave., 456-2010
*M—Fine Marin County French that "can sometimes be
wonderful, but you never know"; though it's "slipped a bit"
and has mundane decor and occasionally haughty service, it
still has the "best French food in Marin".*

Max's Diner | 15 | 20 | 18 | $13 |
311 3rd St. (near Folsom St.), 546-0168
*M—Campy '50s diner that reviewers either love or hate; the
waitresses wear bobby socks and pink poodle dog skirts;
though the American food won't win any prizes, the portions
are large; fans call it "campy fun"; foes say it's a "nut house,
not a dining experience".*

Max's Opera Cafe/LS | 17 | 19 | 16 | $14 |
601 Van Ness Ave. (at Golden Gate Ave.), 771-7300
*M—The location of this deli (smack in the heart of Civic
Center) scores most points—"useful as a place to meet"; the
sandwiches and salads also get praise, but the rest of the food
is to snore over; packed before and after local events.*

	F	D	S	C

Maxwell's Plum/LS | 13 | 22 | 15 | $20 |
900 North Point (at Ghirardelli Sq.), 441-4140
*M—Like its NYC sibling, this restaurant/circus misses on
food, but scores for its "great view" and "kitschy" decor;
some say the kitchen has "the palate sensitivity of a horse";
however, others have sensed some improvement.*

MEADOWOOD (St. Helena) | 23 | 25 | 21 | $26 |
900 Meadowood Lane, 707-963-3646
*M—California Nouvelle in a dazzling environment
overlooking a golf course; though not universally praised,
presentation is normally beautiful and the food delicious;
service is attentive and likable; stay overnight.*

Mekong*/SX | 21 | 10 | 15 | $9 |
730 Larkin Ave. (near O'Farrell St.), 928-8989
*U—Civic Center Vietnamese that gets high marks for
food, but low ones for ambiance; "everyone smoked,
including the waiter"; a "dive", recommended for cheap
and filling lunches.*

Mesa/S (Oakland) | 21 | 20 | 21 | $20 |
3909 Grand Ave., 652-5223
*M—California cuisine that most call "excellent", but others
call "boring"; it has clean "yuppie-pretty" decor and decent
service that can be "dunderheaded at times".*

Mifune*/S | 19 | 15 | 15 | $9 |
1737 Post St. (at Webster Ave.), 922-0337
*U—Japantown noodle house that gets high marks for—you
guessed it—noodles; no decor to speak of, but it's pleasant
enough; cheap and fast; it's comparable to "McDonald's
Japanese style."*

Mikado/SX (Berkeley) | – | – | – | I |
6228 Telegraph Ave. (near 63rd St.), 654-1000
*East Bay Japanese that offers good sushi and other Nippon
dishes; local college kids love it; fresh and refreshing;
bargain prices.*

Mike's Chinese Cuisine/S | 20 | 14 | 17 | $13 |
5145 Geary Blvd. (at 15th Ave.), 752-0120
*M—Popular Richmond district Cantonese; following
redecorating, many say quality wavered; some love
the "mild" food and say this is their "favorite Chinese";
others find the cuisine "bland" and "ordinary" with "too
much MSG".*

Milano Pizzeria*/X | 21 | 15 | 18 |\$14 |

1330 Ninth Ave. (at Geary Blvd.), 665-3773
*U—Popular Richmond area pizza parlor that reviewers call "a
real steal for great crusty pizza and fresh ingredients"; not
much to look at, but very friendly.*

Milly's/S (San Rafael) | 20 | 16 | 17 |\$12 |

1613 Fourth St., 459-1601
*U—Hotshot Marin county vegetarian that is loved even by
staunch carnivores—"the best presentation I've ever
experienced", "wonderful, even if you're not into health food".*

MIRAMONTE/X (St. Helena) | 28 | 24 | 23 |\$35 |

1327 Railroad Ave., 707-963-3970
*M—"Magnifique!" French Nouvelle restaurant that has
garnered a curious mix of reviews reflecting excellent,
skillfully prepared food and snobby service; "it would be so
pleasant without the arrogance"; high prices and no credit
cards—ridiculous! But with food this good (close on the heels
of Masa's), you'll hear few complaints.*

Miz Brown's Feed Bag/SX | 8 | 5 | 12 | \$8 |

731 Clement St. (at 7th Ave.), 752-5017
*U—Old-time Richmond district coffee shop that doesn't rate
any cheers; campy, but "not much to recommend it"; "great
slumming" if you can stand "very old grease".*

Modesto Lanzone's/LS | 22 | 25 | 20 |\$25 |

601 Van Ness Ave. (at Golden Gate Ave.), 928-0400
900 North Point (at Ghirardelli Sq.), 771-2880
*M—Popular Northern Italian with two locations; pastas and
veal specialties that are highly touted; the Van Ness outlet
gets better ratings, especially for its fine collection of
contemporary art; service is attentive and prices high.*

Monroe's/L | 21 | 20 | 22 |\$25 |

1968 Lombard St. (at Webster St.), 567-4550
*U—Small, charming, Continental restaurant that has
become a local institution; "a bit dusty and old-fashioned,
but pleasant"; most reviewers like the dark ambiance and
friendly service.*

MUSTARD'S GRILL/S | 24 | 19 | 21 |\$21 |

(Yountville)
7399 St. Helena Highway, 707-944-2424
*U—This trendy California cuisine "oasis" on the wine trail is
often "crowded, but the food is excellent"; Cindy Pawcyln
(also co-owner of Rio Grill and Fog City Diner) can really
cook up a storm; like any smashing success, it can be a mob
scene and may suffer lapses.*

| | **F** | **D** | **S** | **C** |

Nadine */S (Berkeley) | 23 | 19 | 22 | $19 |
2400 San Pablo Ave. (near Channing Ave.), 549-2807
*U—Too often "overlooked" East Bay Continental; it's
nothing exceptional, just good cooking in a comfortable
setting at a fair price.*

Napoli * | 19 | 14 | 22 | $14 |
2435 Clement St. (at 26th Ave.), 752-3003
*U— "Delightful" little Richmond district Southern Italian
place where the "veal pizzaiolla is always excellent"; simple,
but pleasant with friendly service.*

Narai/S | 21 | 13 | 15 | $13 |
2229 Clement St. (at 24th Ave.), 751-6363
*U—Unusual and delicious combination of Thai and Chinese
in Richmond district; decor doesn't equal the exceptionally
good food; still, this place is busy, often with a wait, but the
service is always friendly.*

Narsai's Cafe/S | 18 | 14 | 15 | $14 |
135 Stockton St. (at Geary Blvd.), 362-2100
*M—In I. Magnin department store; Downtown shoppers' pit
stop offering salads, sandwiches and gooey desserts; many
praise the convenience and "delicious cafe food"; some are
not amused—"the food looks good, but isn't".*

Neon Chicken/LS | 22 | 19 | 21 | $15 |
4063 18th St. (near Castro St.), 863-0484
*U—A bright, homey spot offering "chicken specialties with
outstanding and unusual sauces"; our reviewers praise the
service, consistency and reasonable prices; "the loveliest bar
in town".*

New Joe's/L | 16 | 13 | 14 | $13 |
347 Geary Blvd. (at Union Sq.), 989-6733
*U—Big brother of the other "Joe" places around town; you
get big burgers, pasta and grilled foods; counter service;
convenient when shopping.*

New San Remo/LS | 17 | 19 | 19 | $16 |
2237 Mason St. (at Chestnut St.), 673-9090
*U—Eighty-year-old North Beach (dinner only) Italian that
draws praise for "reliable food", "fun old SF atmosphere",
"great squid appetizers", good service and reasonable prices.*

	F	D	S	C

Nicaragua Restaurant */LSX | 16 | 6 | 15 | $9 |
3015 Mission St. (at Army St.), 826-3672
*U—Mission district Latin American standby offering "good
cheap food especially seafood"; despite a bad location and
grubby decor, the food is "unusual" and inexpensive; "don't
miss the yucca" or the "best ceviche for miles".*

Nikko Sushi/LS | 18 | 17 | 17 | $16 |
1450 Van Ness Ave. (at Pine St.), 474-7722
*U—Old-time establishment Japanese that serves a
dressier, older crowd; excellent sushi and a full menu
of cooked foods too; sit on the floor or dine western
style; elegant and attractive.*

Nob Hill Cafe/LX | 22 | 17 | 21 | $22 |
1152 Taylor St. (near Clay St.), 776-6915
*M—Around the corner from the Fairmont Hotel; this tiny
neighborhood spot offers "intimate atmosphere and eclectic
culinary creations"; the "personalized service" has resulted in
a loyal following; expect "delicious, different food".*

Nob Hill Restaurant/LS | – | – | – | E |
1 Nob Hill (at Mason St.), 391-9362
*Attractive, paneled room in the Mark Hopkins Hotel; the
serious California Nouvelle cuisine usually succeeds, with
pastries that are exceptional and a wine list with entries from
all over the United States.*

Norman's Restaurant/S | 18 | 18 | 19 | $20 |
(Berkeley)
3204 College Ave. (at Alcatraz Ave.), 655-5291
*M—Small East Bay Nouvelle Californian that some reviewers
call "innovative", but others say "does not meet the test";
service can be a bit spaced out.*

North Beach Restaurant/LS | 17 | 14 | 16 | $11 |
1512 Stockton St. (off Columbus Ave.), 392-1587
*M—Old-time North Beach Italian that "hasn't changed much
from the '50s"; its "seafood is good, pasta mediocre";
operated on a mass feeding level, this antiquated hangout is
"a second choice"; "the decor may generate indigestion".*

North India Restaurant/LS | 22 | 17 | 19 | $18 |
3131 Webster Ave. (near Lombard St.), 931-1556
*U—Exotic Indian curries and tandoories are roundly applauded
as the "best Indian food in the city"; run by a charming family,
their care and hard work show in the fine food and service;
"dine early before the crowds".*

	F	D	S	C

Ocean/S | 20 | 8 | 13 | $13 |

726 Clement St. (near 8th Ave.), 221-3351
239 Clement St. (near Fourth Ave.), 668-1688
U—Popular, bustling Richmond district Cantonese featuring seafood; our surveyors love this place; many "will eat here any day, any time, any thing"; except for its ambiance, that is non-existent, this place is a deal and a half.

Ocean City | – | – | – | I |

644 Broadway (at Kearny St.), 982-2328
One of the largest and busiest dim sum parlors in San Francisco; lots of action, some of it the wrong kind, where Chinatown meets Bawdway.

Old Swiss House/S | 19 | 19 | 20 | $18 |

Pier 39 (at Fisherman's Wharf), 434-0432
U—A Swiss country-style chalet incongruously located in the midst of touristy Pier 39; many praise the food, especially fondues and Old World decor, but for some "nothing is worth having to endure Pier 39".

Olema Inn, The/S (Olema) | – | – | – | M |

10,000 Sir Francis Drake Blvd., 663-8441
Marin County romantic inn by the sea; its innovative American cooking includes many dishes based on fresh oysters, local seafood and organic vegetables; people like the Library Bar.

Omnivore */S (Berkeley) | 20 | 15 | 19 | $19 |

3015 Shattuck Ave. (near Ashby Ave.), 848-4346
U—Open-kitchen East Bay Continental specializing in fresh fish and smoked lamb; the "artistic, imaginative food" gets consistent praise; moderately priced for what it is.

Ondine/LS (Sausalito) | 18 | 22 | 18 | $24 |

558 Bridgeway St., 332-0791
M—Great views of SF across the water are universally applauded, but the Continental food draws mixed notices; some say "good seafood", while others call the menu "pricey and overrated"; expect "more tourists than locals".

Original Joe's/LS | 18 | 11 | 16 | $13 |

144 Taylor St. (near Turk St.), 775-4877
U—After 50 years, this Italian-American is still a deal, if not a treat; you'll get "quantity with occasional quality"; "osso bucco on Wednesdays—yum", "corned beef on Thursdays—to die for", great burgers and thick steaks; it's "cheap and filling"; the ancient waiters are part of the charm.

	F	**D**	**S**	**C**

Orsi/L | 19 | 18 | 18 | $23 |

375 Bush St. (at Kearny St.), 981-6535
*U—Old, stuffy Northern Italian to be sure, but nonetheless
there are some notable specials—"ask for the veal dishes
not on the menu"; ornate, windowless decor; the check
mounts up.*

Osome/LS | 24 | 16 | 19 | $20 |

1923 Fillmore St. (at Pine St.), 346-2311
*U—Popular for sushi with skilled chefs and patient waiters;
"Chef Toshi is a wild man; order from him at the bar"; an
old-timer, but still one of the best sushi-yas in San Francisco.*

Pacific Cafe/LSX | – | – | – | M |

7000 Geary Blvd. (at 34th Ave.), 387-7091
*Seafood only; this Richmond district place gets high marks
for good economical specials; popularity and a no-reservation
policy cause lines, but the food is worth the wait; dinner only.*

Pacific Heights Bar & Grill/LS | 19 | 21 | 20 | $19 |

2001 Fillmore St. (at Pine St.), 567-3337
*U— "Yuppieville", yes, but really good; one of the best
selections of fresh oysters and seafood in SF; "I was
surprisingly impressed—not a typical SF place; the food
is special"; check out the pastas and the interesting
Sunday brunch.*

Palm, The/LS | 17 | 16 | 17 | $21 |

586 Bush St. (at Stockton St.), 981-1222
*M—This local rendition of the famous New York steak house
is not up to the original; the steaks can be very good and
there's a good selection of large, fresh Maine lobsters and
delicious fried onion rings, but as the above ratings reflect,
it could be disappointing.*

Paolo's * (San Jose) | 21 | 20 | 19 | $22 |

520 East Santa Clara St., 408-294-2558
*M—Reviewers praise this casual South Bay place—all love
the views, some love the food; steaks draw raves, but some
say the kitchen "tries, but never really hits the mark".*

Paprika's Fono/LS | 16 | 19 | 18 | $17 |

900 North Point (at Ghirardelli Sq.), 441-1223
*M—Hungarian tourist stop in Ghirardelli Square that gets a
lukewarm reception; "microwaved, except for the view";
friendly service and great "fried peasant bread"; always
crowded at lunch.*

Parma/LS
3314 Steiner St. (near Lombard St.), 567-0500
U—Tiny, cozy Italian near Union Street; garlic is everywhere and the service gets rahs; "a fun place!"

Pasha/LS
1516 Broadway (near Van Ness Ave.), 885-4477
M—Van Ness Moroccan that tastes "good; basic and unassuming"; belly dancing and finger food make this "fun for a group".

Pavilion Room/S (Berkeley)
41 Tunnel Rd. (near Ashby Ave.), 843-3000
California cuisine in the Claremont Hotel; great views of SF and the Bay are praised; otherwise the food and the service get ho-hums.

Peacock Restaurant, The/S
2800 Van Ness Ave. (at Lombard St.), 928-7001
M—Reviewers are equally divided about this Indian; some say the food is "fabulous", but others complain that the place is "living on its reputation"; they also cite "sloppy service"; it's still a full house so people must like it.

Perry's/LS
1944 Union St. (near Laguna St.), 922-9022
U—SF's quintessential hangout; this clubby all-American preppy bar has a backslapping, electric atmosphere, "good drinks, good chili, and lots of noise"; there's no better place for burgers or late night hash and to see the natives in their natural habitat.

Phnom Penh
631 Larkin St. (near Eddy St.), 775-5979
Superb Cambodian cuisine is found in this clean, pleasant Angkor Wat sibling; the same family shows the same care and cooking skill serving delicate and delicious dishes; the restaurant is charming, but its location at the edge of SF's Tenderloin neighborhood isn't.

PIERRE AT MERIDIEN
50 3rd St. (near Market St.), 974-6400
M—Some call this fancy Classic French "a flawless dining experience", while others say it's "haughty", "overpriced and precious"; the consensus is definitely positive, with many noting great improvement over the past year; the decor is elegant.

	F	D	S	C

Pier 23 Cafe/SX | 18 | 13 | 16 | $14 |

Pier 23 (at the Embarcadero), 362-5125
*U—Simple waterfront place with good food and value; "fun
and funky, it doesn't try to be something it isn't"; "lovely patio
dining when it's sunny", plus Sunday and nighttime jazz;
"very SF—without forcing it"; lunch only.*

Pietro's/L | 20 | 21 | 20 | $14 |

1851 Union St. (near Octavia St.), 563-4157
*U—Quiet, reasonably priced Italian incongruously
located in a hot, go-go locale; romantic and very low-key;
"great pastas".*

Pixley Cafe/LS | 18 | 17 | 18 | $15 |

3127 Fillmore St. (near Greenwich St.), 346-6123
*U—Yuppie-ish "brass and glass cafe" that's often overlooked,
especially for lunch; it's got "nice neighborhood fare",
"nothing exciting, but convenient"; a good place to feed
when doing Union Street.*

Plearn Thai Cuisine/S (Berkeley) | 23 | 16 | 16 | $13 |

2050 University Ave. (near Shattuck Ave.), 841-2148
*U—Bay Area's best Thai has "great food" (for the asbestos
palate set) and simple, but attractive decor; offering a
remarkable variety of tastes and flavors, it's always busy;
"the wait can be ridiculous".*

Post Street Bar & Cafe | – | – | – | M |

632 Post St. (near Jones St.), 928-2080
*"Excellent and reliable"; the California-style seafood here
is fresh and delicious, the soups are first-rate, but the
place has never gotten the kudos it deserves; attractive and
reasonably priced.*

Prego Ristorante/LS | 20 | 19 | 17 | $18 |

2000 Union St. (at Buchanan St.), 563-3305
*U—Chic trattoria—trendy to the max, crowded to the max
and still it's good; gets bravos for pricey pastas and pizza; a
no-reservation policy packs the bar; "if you need a weekend
date, go Friday afternoon".*

Raf/S | – | – | – | E |

478 Green St. (near Grant Ave.), 362-1999
*Large, interestingly decorated and comfortable newcomer
serving modern Northern Italian fare; hip and trendy, this
casually elegant North Beach spot features grilled game,
unusual pastas and a daily risotto special; service is friendly if
a bit precious.*

	F	**D**	**S**	**C**

Ramona (San Rafael) | – | – | – | I |

1025 C St. (near 4th St.), 454-0761
*On good nights, this Mexican, with great chicken mole, can
be one of the best in the Bay Area; on bad nights, adios
amigos; tacky decor is offset by the guitarist's romantic notes.*

Restaurant 101/L | 22 | 22 | 20 | $30 |

101 California St. (at Front St.), 788-4101
*M—Swank, French Nouvelle; applause for "simply
wonderful food served in a beautifully dramatic setting" and
"elegant and refined, yet adventurous, cuisine" is mixed with
comments such as "lots of misses, but some highs" and
"damn, it's expensive".*

Restaurant Rodin/L | – | – | – | E |

1779 Lombard St. (near Laguna St.), 563-8566
*Fancy French Nouvelle newcomer reportedly offers elegant
ambiance and beautiful food.*

Riera's (Berkeley) | 20 | 15 | 19 | $16 |

1539 Solano Ave. (at Nielson St.), 527-1467
*M—East Bay Italian owned by restaurant critic Russ Riera
and his family; some find the food "tasty and soul satisfying"
and call the place "a little gem", but others cite "grumpy"
service and say Riera's needs work—"critic, critique thyself!"*

Rings | 21 | 14 | 19 | $19 |

1131 Folsom St. (near 8th St.), 621-2111
*M—Hot spot in the SOMA that is still feeling its way; despite
many positive reviews, its original California cuisine
sometimes falls flat; the high noise level and funky setting
rankle as many as they excite; nonetheless, this is definitely
"where it's at."*

Rio Grill/LS (Carmel) | 24 | 20 | 20 | $19 |

101 Crossroads Blvd., 408-625-5436
*U—Modern, spirited Carmel branch of the Mustard's—
Fog City triumvirate; its youthful ambiance and clever
California food work well—most of the time; Chef Cindy
Pawlcyn divides her time between the three places, and her
imaginative hand is visible throughout the menu; affable
service; good wine list.*

Ristorante Fabrizio/L (Larkspur) | 21 | 15 | 21 | $17 |

455 Magnolia Ave., 924-3332
*U—Many Marinites say this is "a rising star", praising the
large Italian menu and the "thoughtful service"; some say
dishes can be mediocre, but most call this crowded place
"a favorite".*

	F	D	S	C

Ristorante Grifone/LS | – | – | – | M |

1609 Powell St. (at Green St.), 397-8458
Busy North Beach Italian where "reservations don't seem to mean much", so be patient—what you're waiting for is "the best gnocchi al gorgonzola" and other fine pastas; the rest is "so-so" in a "Godfather-style setting".

Ronayne's/S | 15 | 15 | 17 | $17 |

1799 Lombard St. (at Laguna St.), 922-5060
M—Seafood near the Marina, gets ho-hums from our reviewers; e.g. "used to be a good restaurant", "it's stale"; on the plus side, mussels and calamari are frequently praised; comfortable and attractive.

Rosalie's/LS | 18 | 23 | 17 | $25 |

1415 Van Ness Ave. (near Pine St.), 928-7188
M—Stylish Californian that is "inconsistent but moving in the right direction" and is "great for people-watching late at night"; tin palm trees and tin tables (really) highlight a trendy setting that is "fun to see".

ROSE ET LAFAVOUR'S | 25 | 22 | 23 | $41 |
CAFE ORIENTAL/S (St. Helena)

1420 Main St., 707-963-1681
M—Touted Nouvelle chef Bruce Lafavour recently changed the menu and added 'Cafe Oriental' to emphasize his Asian influences; many say the "changes are good" and "when this place is on, it's great", even if "a bit precious"; a fine wine list, too.

Rotunda, The | 17 | 24 | 17 | $19 |

150 Stockton St. (at Geary Blvd.), 362-4777
U—The ladies who lunch can be found at this Neiman Marcus watering spot; "good yakkity-yak shopping stop for rich ladies"; assessments of the spectacular setting range from "elegant" to "pretentious"; the pricey California food, designed for the diet-conscious, is surprisingly good.

Samantha's/L | 20 | 21 | 21 | $22 |

1265 Battery St. (near Greenwich St.), 986-0100
U—Dark wood-paneled Downtown tavern serving "light interpretations of Cajun cuisine with a California touch"; there are plenty of "good Creole specials" and "sensational breads"; service is good and most see "lots of potential".

Sam's Anchor Cafe/LS (Tiburon) | 15 | 18 | 14 | $13 |

27 Main St. (at Tiburon Blvd.), 435-4527
U—Drop anchor at this Marin seafood spot if you can sit on the deck for "brunch and people-watching"; the kitchen gets no raves, but the setting is so delightful, most reviewers are very forgiving; "great views".

	F	D	S	C

Sam's Grill & Seafood | 21 | 16 | 17 | $17 |
374 Bush St. (near Kearny St.), 421-0594
*U—Downtown tradition for "consistently good seafood"; "an
old-time favorite" particularly at lunch; the "no-nonsense
service" feels "crusty" to some; regulars get preference—if
you're not one, your reservation could get lost.*

Samurai * /S (Sausalito) | 21 | 17 | 16 | $14 |
2633 Bridgeway St., 332-8245
*U—Reviewers call this the "best sushi bar in Marin"; besides
being attractive and a good value, it's "clean" and "fun";
"the samurai dinner is more than one person can handle";
kids love it.*

Sand Dollar * /SX (Stinson Beach) | 17 | 13 | 17 | $13 |
3458 Highway 7, 868-0434
*U—A small and "casual" seaside hangout for the Marin
locals; adequate if you're famished and don't feel like driving;
don't expect much, just decent sandwiches, okay salads and
a pleasant outdoor setting.*

San Francisco Bar-B-Que /S | 21 | 9 | 15 | $11 |
1328 18th St. (near Missouri St.), 431-8956
*U—Potrero Hill Thai barbecue that's "terrific" and "cheap";
this "hole-in-the-wall" is a far cry from a complete dining
experience, but it's a wonderful bargain; with such top quality
food at minimal prices, you must expect a wait to get in.*

Sanppo Restaurant /S | 21 | 11 | 16 | $12 |
1702 Post St. (at Buchanan St.), 346-3486
*U—Japantown place that gets compliments for its food and
raves for its prices; the decor is unremarkable, but overall, it
can be relied on for "good standard Japanese food at below
standard prices."*

Sante Fe Bar & Grill /LS | 22 | 20 | 18 | $23 |
(Berkeley)
1310 University Ave. (near Acton St.), 841-4740
*M—Jeremiah Tower's East Bay stepping-stone to the Stars
offers clever California cuisine in a hip noisy atmosphere
that's "jazzy" and "fun"; the place is "so trendy, even the
waiters don't know what's going on"; only "sometimes
excellent", the food has gotten "better in recent months".*

Sardine Factory /LS (Monterey) | 17 | 21 | 19 | $26 |
701 Wave St., 408-373-3775
*M—Monterey's top tourist destination gets only a lukewarm
endorsement for its food; our respondents think the kitchen
"needs to try harder"; the ambiance is "elegant" to some and
"garish" to others; everyone agrees the service is very good
and the wine list superb.*

Savannah Grill/LS
(Corte Madera)
55 Tamal Vista Blvd. (near Lucky Drive), 924-6770
*M — Mustard's Marin County "clone" is off to a fast start
serving a big, noisy, occasionally "rowdy", yuppie crowd; a
clever Cal-cuisine menu is packing them in, but our
surveyors, despite giving plus marks to the food, complain
that sometimes the kitchen misses.*

Schroeder's
240 Front St. (near California St.), 421-4778
*U — 1893 landmark financial district German that gets kudos
for reliability and hearty meat and potatoes "stick to your
ribs" fare; it's an "oldie-but-goodie" and "a value"; the
sauerbraten at lunch on Tuesday and Friday gets raves.*

S. Asimakopoulous
288 Connecticut St. (at 18th St.), 552-8789
*Many feel this is the best place in town for Greek food —
"fantastic lamb" was noted several times by our surveyors;
off the beaten track in the Potrero Hill area, but worth trying
to pronounce — and find.*

Scoma's/LS
Pier 47 (near Jefferson St.), 771-4383
2421 Larkspur Landing Circle, Larkspur, 461-6161
588 Bridgeway St., Sausalito, 332-9551
*"Good fish, even though the tourists school here"; good,
honest food at a decent price, plus professional and friendly
service, win this seafood house the highest praise of any on
Fisherman's Wharf; the Sausalito branch is good too.*

Scott's Seafood Grill & Bar/LS
2400 Lombard St. (at Scott St.), 563-8988
3 Embarcadero Ctr., 433-7444
73 Jack London Sq., Oakland, 444-3456
2300 E. Bayshore Rd., Palo Alto, 856-1046
*M — "Decent, but why the crowd? It's not that good"; what
started as a good spot for basic seafood, is now a Bay Area
chain living precariously on its laurels; many call the food
"bland" and "overpriced"; of the branches, Palo Alto gets the
best notices and Oakland the worst.*

Sears Fine Foods/SX
439 Powell St. (near Post St.), 986-1160
*U — Popular '50s era breakfast spot; "tacky and crowded, but
great breakfasts"; "in and out quick"; "superb waitresses are
just like mom"; often a wait for lunch and, over the years, has
become "something of a tourist draw"; no dinner.*

Seoul Garden/S — | – | – | – | I |
22 Peace Plaza (in Japantown), 563-7664
*Authentic Korean place that offers exotic dishes grilled right
at the table; service is by diffident kimonoed ladies and the
decor is attractive; particularly suited to groups of six; kids
enjoy it.*

Shadows, The/S — | 15 | 20 | 16 | $23 |
1349 Montgomery St. (at Filbert St.), 982-5536
*U— "Great view, but this contemporary French needs
better food"; declined after it had a facelift and a management
change; romantic and beautiful, but you may have to put up
with rude help; will it improve? only The Shadow knows.*

Sharl's/S (Sonoma) — | 20 | 16 | 19 | $17 |
136 West Napa, 707-996-5155
*U— "Traditional dining place" that gets moderate praise for
good Continental food; friendly, attentive service almost
makes up for the "outdated green decor".*

Siam Cuisine/LS (Berkeley) — | 20 | 13 | 17 | $13 |
1181 University Ave. (near San Pablo Ave.), 548-3278
*U— Top-notch Thai with a wide variety of excellent "hot
stuff"; "tacky cocktail lounge surroundings" are unfortunate,
but not fatal; at these prices, it's a steal.*

South China Cafe */S — | 11 | 5 | 15 | $11 |
4133 18th St. (at Castro St.), 861-9323
*U— "MSG reigns" in this drab Castro district luncheonette; a
neighborhood "greasy spoon", it serves barely adequate
Chinese food fast and cheap.*

Spenger's Fish Grotto/LS — | 13 | 11 | 12 | $13 |
(Berkeley)
1919 4th St. (at University Ave.), 845-7771
*U— "Overpriced, overrated, overcrowded"; a holdover from
the days when SF was a major fishing port, this busy fish
factory is best for tiny kids and grandparents; "cheap and it
shows—the food's awful"; mediocrity for the masses.*

Spuntino/L — | – | – | – | I |
524 Van Ness Ave. (near McAllister St.), 861-7772
*Italian snacks right near the Civic Center concert halls; it's a
jazzy attractive scene with pizzas, sandwiches, salads, pastas,
plus breezy service; a hangout.*

| F | D | S | C |

SQUARE ONE/S | 24 | 18 | 20 | $26 |
190 Pacific St. (at Front St.), 788-1110
U—Among the Bay's best multi-ethnic places; Chef-owner Joyce Goldstein perfected her grillmanship at Chez Panisse; her incredible homebaked breads and "original food will perk up the most jaded palate"; the few complaints we hear center on "sterile" decor and abrupt service, but the consensus is that this culinary adventure is "great fun".

Squid's Cafe/LS | 14 | 14 | 13 | $13 |
96 McAllister St. (at Leavenworth St.), 861-0100
U—For "every calamari concoction possible" and a loud jukebox, this is the place, but you'd better like pink punk and a "rather strange staff"; the menu offers "deep-fried everything" and a terminal case of "garlic breath".

Squire Restaurant */S | 26 | 26 | 23 | $30 |
950 Mason St. (at California St.), 772-5211
U—Traditional, fancy-pants Continental in a serene setting in the legendary Fairmont Hotel; you'll get highly professional service and surprisingly good (if unimaginative) food; pretentious and pricey, it's very impressive nonetheless.

Stanford Park Hotel * | 15 | 18 | 14 | $22 |
(Menlo Park)
100 El Camino Real, 324-1234
U—Peninsula American restaurant that tries to impress with elegance and high prices, but doesn't deliver the goods; attractive, but needs work.

STARS/LS | 24 | 21 | 21 | $27 |
1050 Redwood St. (off Van Ness Ave.), 861-7827
U—Celebrated Chef Jeremiah Tower's "in place" is a cosmopolitan brasserie with a dash of elegance; a temple of California cuisine, this "trend-setting" Civic Center hangout always bustles; some say service is "spotty" and food "inconsistent"; but this has some of the cleverest and most creative cooking in the country, especially when Tower is on the scene.

Station House Cafe (Point Reyes) | 22 | 13 | 18 | $14 |
11285 State Highway 1, 663-1515
U—A casual roadhouse serving "outstanding" eclectic California food; this obscure small town cafe is a regular stop for locals, bikers and families that are hip to a good value; definitely worth the drive.

Sugar's Grill & Sushi Bar/LS | 17 | 15 | 17 | $18 |
1785 Union St. (at Octavia St.), 776-2929
M—For undecided (or daring) appetites, this curious East-West combination of sushi, cooked fish and pastas may be the thing; some say they are "doing too many things", but it's "new" and "innovative" and probably "needs time" to work out the kinks.

63

	F	D	S	C

Sushi Gen/S | 20 | 15 | 16 | $17 |
4248 18th St. (at Diamond St.), 864-2197
*M—A Noe Valley sushi bar that has seen better days;
although our reviewers were entertained by the chefs, they
found the sushi a bit tired and "uninspired"; small and
sometimes crowded.*

Sutter 500/S | 23 | 17 | 19 | $29 |
500 Sutter St. (at Powell St.), 362-3346
*M—Changes have rocked this establishment; though the cafe
is a "glorified coffee shop", the restaurant behind it is serene
and elegant; however, Chef Hubert Keller, whose fine French
cooking won this restaurant's high ratings, has split for Fleur
de Lys; be wary, things are in flux here.*

Swan Oyster Depot | 24 | 12 | 20 | $13 |
1517 Polk St. (near California St.), 673-1101
*U—Legendary, atmospheric seafood bar complete with
sawdust on the floor and "the best oysters and clam chowder
in SF"; for regulars and tourists alike, "this is the kind of place
that gives SF its character"; no dinner.*

TADICH GRILL | 22 | 18 | 18 | $17 |
240 California St. (near Battery St.), 391-2373
*M—A true SF institution loaded with crusty antique charm;
expect classic grill fare with top-quality ingredients simply
prepared; it may be slipping a little; service can be brusque
and the wait at lunch can be long…very long.*

Taiwan Restaurant * (Berkeley) | 16 | 8 | 11 | $10 |
2071 University Ave. (near Shattuck Ave.), 845-1456
*U— "Standard Chinese" in a clean, but dull, East Bay setting;
the Taiwanese food is served so quickly that it's to the point of
being "rushed".*

Taqueria Mission | – | – | – | I |
4798 Mission St. (at 28th St.), 469-5053
*This place has it all—great tacos, burritos and wonderful
Mexican fruit drinks; it's a gas in more ways than one.*

Taqueria Tepatitlan */SX | 20 | 5 | 15 | $6 |
2198 Folsom St. (at 18th St.), 626-1499
*U— "A lunch made in heaven"; grand lamb burritos and
crunchy flautas; not much to look at, but what a bargain!*

	F	D	S	C

Tien Fu | 19 | 10 | 15 | $11 |

1395 Noriega St. (at 21st Ave.), 665-1064
3945 24th St. (near Noe St.), 282-9502
U—Outstanding Chinese dishes keep this place busy in spite of the "dirty", neglected decor; "a real bargain, great vegie food, good service"; the garlic chicken and the green onion pancakes are "incredible".

Tokyo Sukiyaki */LS | 22 | 23 | 22 | $22 |

225 Jefferson St. (at Taylor St.), 775-9030
U—An innocuous Fisherman's Wharf Japanese lunch spot that you'll forget before dinnertime; decent and attractive; slow service.

Tommaso's/LS | 22 | 13 | 17 | $14 |

1042 Kearny St. (at Broadway), 398-9696
U—At this North Beach pizza joint you will be totally satisfied if you stick to the pizza; you'll also be extra hungry after the wait to get in; but the "great pizzas from woodburning ovens" are worth it.

Ton Kiang/LS | 21 | 9 | 15 | $11 |

3148 Geary Blvd. (at Spruce St.), 752-4440
5827 Geary Blvd. (at 23rd Ave.), 386-8530
(Check phone book for other locations.)
U—Northern Chinese (Hakka) bargain with plastic decor that gets warmer with each new location; all branches are busy and rushed, but service is friendly and any discomfort is manageable considering the food quality; try the great spareribs and black bean steamed oysters.

TRADER VIC'S/LS | 17 | 22 | 19 | $28 |

20 Cosmo Place (off Taylor St.), 776-2232
9 Anchor Dr. (Emeryville), 653-3400
M—Polynesian tourist mecca that's showing its age; "sweet and sour cobwebs"; exotic "island" drinks with fanciful names outshine anything on the menu; the classy "Captain's Cabin" is a ladies-who-lunch hangout and the Polynesian rooms are a hit with the kids.

Trattoria Contadina/LS | 18 | 13 | 16 | $15 |

1800 Mason St. (at Union St.), 982-5728
M—Small family storefront with Tuscan food that's usually good, but not always; "charming" and "homey", it's a casual, friendly place.

Trio Cafe/SX | – | – | – | I |

1870 Fillmore St. (near Bush St.), 563-2248
Open for lunch only, this Pacific Heights spot charms many with its fresh, homemade sandwiches; besides tables, it has a stand-up counter for quickie lunches.

	F	D	S	C

Tu Lan Restaurant *
| | 21 | 6 | 16 | $6 |

8 Sixth St. (at Market St.), 626-0927
U—Very good Vietnamese food in one of the worst neighborhoods in town and with decor to match; bring a bodyguard.

Tung Fong/S
| | 24 | 9 | 16 | $11 |

808 Pacific Ave. (at Stockton St.), 362-7115
U—It's Shanghai dim sum and good, with "the greatest steamed buns in SF", and that's saying a lot; "the roast crab is sensational"; a strong contender for the city's best dim sum; no dinners.

Umberto's/L
| | 19 | 21 | 18 | $21 |

141 Steuart St. (near Mission St.), 543-8021
U—An out-of-the-way Northern Italian, "romantic" charmer with a piano bar; "very good for its size and scope"; the waiters are most "helpful", and the food's good too.

Upstart Crow & Company
| | 12 | 14 | 11 | $10 |

2801 Leavenworth St. (at Green St.), 474-3822
M—A combination restaurant-book store that might work "if it were better managed"; as is, "service stinks" and, as one reviewer suggests, this coffee shop "shoulda stuck with just books!"

U.S. Restaurant/X
| | 15 | 9 | 15 | $11 |

431 Columbus Ave. (near Green St.), 362-6251
M—Simple, homey Southern Italian storefront that is "reasonably priced and unpretentious"; some praise the big portions and "plain" food, but others aren't so sure.

Vanessi's/L
| | 18 | 13 | 15 | $18 |

498 Broadway (at Kearny St.), 421-0890
1177 California St. (near Jones St.), 771-2422
M—Longtime local favorite that some feel is "sliding into mediocrity"; yet others report that "solid Italian food" is still available if you know the menu; diners are advised to "sit at the counter" and avoid the "lousy table service".

Vegi Food/SX
| | 21 | 8 | 16 | $10 |

1820 Clement St. (near 19th Ave.), 387-8111
U—Richmond district Asian-influenced vegetarian cafe with a plain-Jane setting; our surveyors give raves to the deep-fried walnuts; "high quality" and "earnest service" have kept this small storefront spot busy.

Via Veneto/L (Oakland) | 15 | 14 | 16 |$14 |
5356 College Ave., 652-8540
*U—Not much to get excited about here; most people say
this decent East Bay Italian place "could be much better";
however, the service is friendly and the ambiance is pleasant.*

Vicolo Pizzeria/LSX | – | – | – | I |
201 Ivy St. (near Grove St.), 776-1331
900 North Point (at Ghirardelli Sq.), 776-1331
*Several pizzaphiles claim this place produces the "best
pizza in the world"; certainly the calzone and deep-dish pizza
are something special; the food is surprisingly upscale and
inventive and the decor is better than the pizzeria norm.*

Victor's/LS | 18 | 22 | 21 |$27 |
335 Powell St. (at Geary Blvd.), 956-7777
*M—More visitors than locals are attracted to this haute
California French restaurant atop the St. Francis Hotel; it
gets mixed reviews: some call it "highly overrated and
overpriced", but the plush ambiance and spectacular views
get raves.*

Vivande Porta Via/S | – | – | – | I |
2125 Fillmore St. (off California St.), 346-4430
*Italian gourmet take-out with tables and counter in the back;
good salads, nice pastas, interesting combinations, all at nice
low prices; lunch only.*

Vlasta's Czechoslovakian | 16 | 12 | 18 |$15 |
2420 Lombard St. (near Scott St.), 931-7533
*U—This Old World Czech place gets raves for its roast duck
and "thoughtful" service, but its heavy Central European
style and large portions deter as many customers as they
endear; consistent, if not brilliant; overall, most think this
place is "worth every cent".*

Warszawa/S | 19 | 18 | 19 |$16 |
1730 Shattuck Ave. (near Francisco Ave.), 841-5539
*U—East Bay Polish place featuring hearty food in a cozy,
romantic setting; attentive service and moderate prices
account for this restaurant's popularity.*

WASHINGTON SQUARE | 19 | 18 | 18 |$19 |
BAR & GRILL /LS
1707 Powell St. (at Union St.), 982-8123
*M—Clubby, power scene saloon called the "WashBag"
by the movers and groovers who happily contribute to its
high levels of "noise, fun and smoke"; despite "mediocre
food" and a "locker room atmosphere", for the locals,
celebs and oglers it's an "all-around good choice"; great jazz
piano in the evenings.*

F	D	S	C

Waterfront Restaurant/LS | – | – | – | M |
Pier 7 Embarcadero (at Broadway), 391-2696
Handsome wood and brass seafood spot with incredible
bridge views; reviewers praise the friendly service and
"excellent fresh seafood", although the preparation
lacks personality.

Yamato Sukiyaki House | 19 | 20 | 20 | $18 |
717 California St. (near Grant St.), 397-3456
U—One of SF's older sushi bars; many say it's now a bit
"stale", but most rate the food "consistently good"; kimonoed
waitresses pad about silently; restful and pleasant.

Yet Wah/LS | 16 | 14 | 16 | $14 |
Pier 39, at the Embarcadero, 434-4430
2140 Clement St., 387-8056
1829 Clement St., 751-1231
300 Turney, Sausalito, 331-3300
(Check phone book for other locations.)
U—Chinese chain that's "seemingly everywhere", but most
consider it nothing special; sort of "Chun King style" or "just
plain old Chinese food"; yet, other Wahs keep opening
around the Bay Area.

Yoshida-Ya/LS | 20 | 20 | 19 | $20 |
2909 Webster St. (off Union St.), 346-3431
U—SF's only yakitori bar serves various grilled goodies on
skewers and multi-course dinners, plus nice sushi and
sashimi; the food could be better at the price, but most praise
this unique and very handsome restaurant.

Yoshi's Japanese/LS (Oakland) | – | – | – | I |
6030 Claremont Ave. (near College Ave.), 652-9200
Oakland's biggest sushi bar offers major jazz performances
upstairs and easy-to-take prices.

Yuet Lee/LSX | 22 | 5 | 10 | $13 |
1300 Stockton St. (near Broadway), 982-6000
U— "If it's 3 AM and you're hungry for Chinese food, this is
the place"; it's got "the best fish in the Bay Area", but, on the
downside, the word "dump" was invented to describe this
restaurant.

| | F | D | S | C |

Zola's/L |21 | 20 | 20 |$25|
1722 Sacramento St. (off Polk St.), 775-3311
*M—Intimate and elegant French cafe with a constantly
changing menu; "tries", but "often misses"; despite
"occasionally inspired food", it gets few raves; service is
"cordial" and "knowledgeable"; prices are a bit high.*

Zuni Cafe/LS |22 | 18 | 18 |$20|
1658 Market St. (near Gough St.), 552-2522
*Eclectic, counter-culture food with service that can be
dunderheaded; the creative California menu isn't always on
target, but is still one of the most innovative in town and is
"getting better all the time"; excellent grilled dishes; a
well-chosen wine list and good values are pleasing bonuses.*

INDEXES TO RESTAURANTS

SPECIAL FEATURES AND APPEALS

TYPES OF CUISINE

American
A la Carte
Alfred's
Alta Mira Hotel
Barnaby's
Big Four
Billboard Cafe
Bill's Place
Brazen Head
Bridge Creek Cafe
Campton Place
Dixie Cafe
Doidge's Kitchen
Elite Cafe, The
Fat Apple's
Faz Restaurant & Bar
Hamburger Mary's
Hard Rock Cafe
Harris' Restaurant
Iron Horse, The
Lily's of San Francisco
Mama's
Mama's Royal Cafe
Max's Diner
Max's Opera Cafe
Miz Brown's Feed Bag
Olema Inn, The
Palm, The
Perry's
Pier 23 Cafe
Samantha's
Sears Fine Foods
Stanford Park Hotel
Station House Cafe

Burmese
Mandalay

Cajun
Dixie Cafe
Elite Cafe, The
Samantha's

Californian
Balboa Cafe
Bay Wolf Cafe
Brad Forrest
Broadway Terrace
Butler's
Cafe Beaujolais

Cafe Bedford
Cafe d'Arts
Cafe Majestic
California Cafe
Casa Madrona
Cheer's Cafe
Chez Panisse
Clement Street Bar/Grill
Courtyard, The
Eichelbaum & Co. Cafe
El Drisco Hotel
Fog City Diner
Four Star Restaurant
Fourth Street Grill
French Laundry
Fresh Cream
Hayes Street Grill
Ironwood Cafe
John Ash & Co.
Knickerbockers
London Wine Bar, The
MacArthur Park
Madrona Manor
Meadowood
Mesa
Mustard's Grill
Narsai's Cafe
Neon Chicken
Nob Hill Restaurant
Norman's Restaurant
Pavilion Room
Pixley Cafe
Post Street Bar/Cafe
Rings
Rio Grill
Rosalie's
Rotunda, The
Santa Fe Bar & Grill
Savannah Grill
Square One
Stars
Sugar's Grill/Sushi Bar
Victor's
Zuni Cafe

Cambodian
Angkor Wat
Cambodia House
Phnom Penh

Chinese

Asia Garden
Celadon, The
China House
China Moon Cafe
China Pavilion
China Station
Chu Lin
Empress of China
Feng Nian
Golden Phoenix
Harbor Village
Hunan Restaurant
Hunan Village
Imperial Palace
Kan's
King of China
Kirin
Mandarin House
Mandarin, The
Mike's Chinese Cuisine
Ocean
Ocean City
South China Cafe
Taiwan Restaurant
Tien Fu
Ton Kiang
Tung Fong
Yet Wah
Yuet Lee

Coffee Houses

Caffe Roma
Trio Cafe
Upstart Crow & Co.

Continental

Alexis
Bella Vista
Cafe Fanny
Cafe Mozart
Carnelian Room
Chambord
Cliff House
Dock, The
Doros
Fournou's Ovens
French Room, The
Gervais
Ivy's
Jack's
Jil's Trianon
Julius' Castle

Lark Creek Inn, The
Maxwell's Plum
Monroe's
Nadine
Nob Hill Cafe
Old Swiss House
Omnivore
Ondine
Paolo's
Sardine Factory
Sharl's
Squire Restaurant

Cuban

Cuba

Czechoslovakian

Vlasta's

Delis

Acropolis Deli
Brothers Deli
Max's Opera Cafe
Vivande Porta Via

Dim Sum

Asia Garden
Fook*
Harbor Village
Hong Kong Tea House*
Ming Palace*
Ocean City*
Tung Fong
Yank Sing*

Diners

Fog City Diner
Max's Diner
Mel's Diner*
Sherman's Cal. Diner*

Eclectic

Square One
Trader Vic's

French Bistro

Au Relais
Cafe Bistro Oyster Bar
Christophe
Daniel's
Guernica

(*Not in Survey)

Lalime's
La Mere Duquesne
Le Candide
Le Central
Le Cyrano
Le Metropole
L'Entrecote de Paris
Le Piano Zinc
Le Rhone
L'Escale
Le St. Tropez
L'Olivier
Zola's

French Classic

Barbarossa
Blue Fox
Calif. Culinary Academy
Caprice, The
Chantilly Restaurant
Ernie's
La Petite Auberge
L'Auberge
Le Camembert
Le Club
Le Domino
Le Marquis
Le Papillon
L'Escargot
L'Etoile
Maurice et Charles
Pierre at Meridien

French Nouvelle

Amelio's
Auberge du Soleil
Chez Michel
Domaine Chandon
Fleur de Lys
Le Castel
Masa's
Miramonte
Restaurant 101
Restaurant Rodin
Rose et Lafavour's
Shadows, The
Sutter 500

German

Beethoven
Schroeder's

Greek

S. Asimakopoulous

Hamburgers

Bill's Place
Fat Apples
Hamburger Mary's
Hard Rock Cafe

Hungarian

Paprika's Fono

Indian

Gaylord
India House
India Place
North India
Peacock, The

Indonesian

Java

Italian

Adriana's
Baci
Basta Pasta
Bruno's
Buca Giovanni
Cafe Riggio
Caffe Quadro
Caffe Sport
Caffe Venezia
Carlo's Italian
Ciao Ristorante
Circolo
Dal Baffo
Da Sandro
Donatello
Ernesto's
Fior d'Italia
Giramonti
Giuliano's
Harry's Bar & Grill
Il Pirata
Jackson Fillmore Trattoria
Kuleto's
La Ginestra
La Pergola
La Traviata
Little Italy
Little Joe's
Lucca Ristorante
Marin Joe's
Milano Pizzeria
Modesto Lanzone's
Napoli
New Joe's

New San Remo
North Beach
Original Joe's
Orsi
Parma
Pietro's
Prego Ristorante
Raf
Riera's
Ristorante Fabrizio
Ristorante Grifone
Spuntino
Tommaso's
Trattoria Contadina
Umberto's
U.S. Restaurant
Vanessi's
Via Veneto
Vivande Porta Via
Washington Sq. Bar/Grill

Japanese

Benihana
Ebisu
Edokko
Goro's Robato
Ino Sushi
Isobune Sushi
Kabuto Sushi
Kansai
Kinokawa
Mifune
Mikado
Nikko Sushi
Osome
Samurai
Sanppo
Sushi Gen
Tokyo Sukiyaki
Yamato Sukiyaki
Yoshida-Ya
Yoshi's

Korean

Hahn's Hibachi
Korea House
Korean Palace
Seoul Garden

Mexican

Cadillac Bar
Cantina, The
Don Ramon's

El Sombrero
El Tapatio
Guaymas
Juan's Place
La Fuente
La Mexicana
La Rondalla
Las Camelias
Las Mananitas
La Taqueria
Ramona
Taqueria Mission
Taqueria Tepatitlan

Middle Eastern

Caravansary

Moroccan

Pasha

Nicaraguan

Nicaragua Restaurant

Pizza

Cafe at Chez Panisse
Cafe Quadro
Caffe Sport
Circolo
Ernesto's
Gray Whale
Milano Pizzeria
Prego Ristorante
Spuntino's
Tommaso's
Vicolo Pizzeria

Polish

Warszawa

Polynesian

Trader Vic's

Russian

Acropolis Deli

Salvadorean

El Tazumal

Seafood

Abalonetti
Adriatic
A. Sabella's
Augusta's

Bentley's
Flynn's Landing
Gertie's Chesapeake Bay
Gulf Coast
Horizons
La Rocca's Oyster Bar
Pacific Cafe
Pacific Hts. Bar & Grill
Ronayne's
Sam's Anchor Cafe
Sam's Grill
Sand Dollar
Scoma's
Scott's Seafood Grill
Spenger's Fish Grotto
Squid's Cafe
Swan Oyster Depot
Tadich Grill
Trader Vic's
Waterfront

Southwest

Dakota Grill & Bar

Spanish

Alejandro's Sociedad
Cafe Tango

Steak Houses

Alfred's
Harris' Restaurant
Palm, The

Thai

Khan Toke Thai
Narai
Plearn Thai Cuisine
San Francisco BBQ
Siam Cuisine

Vegetarian

Diamond Street
Green's
Long Life Vegie House
Milly's
Vegi Food

Vietnamese

Aux Delices
Cordon Bleu Vietnamese
Golden Turtle
Kim's
Mai's
Mekong
Tu Lan Restaurant

LOCATIONS

Castro/Noe

Ironwood Cafe
La Mediterranee
Le Piano Zinc
Little Italy
Neon Chicken
South China Cafe
Sushi Gen
Tien Fu

Chinatown

Asia Garden
Celadon, The
Empress of China
Golden Phoenix
Hunan Restaurant
Hunan Village
Imperial Palace
Kan's
Ocean City
Tung Fong
Yuet Lee

Civic Center

Brad Forrest
Cafe d'Arts
Harry's Bar & Grill
Hayes Street Grill
Ivy's
Max's Opera Cafe
Spuntino
Stars
Vicolo Pizzeria

Downtown

Bentley's
Big Four
Blue Fox
Cafe Bedford
Cafe Mozart
Caffe Quadro
California Cafe Bar/Grill
Calif. Culinary Academy
Campton Place
Caravansary
Carnelian Room
Chambord
China Moon Cafe
Ciao Ristorante
Circolo
Cordon Bleu Vietnamese

Donatello
Doros
Ernie's
Faz Restaurant & Bar
Fleur de Lys
Fog City Diner
Four Star Restaurant
Harbor Village
Hunan Restaurant
India House
Iron Horse, The
Jack's
Jil's Trianon
Julius' Castle
Kansai
Kinokawa
Korean Palace
Kuleto's
La Fuente
La Mere Duquesne
Las Mananitas
Le Candide
Le Central
Lily's of San Francisco
L'Olivier
London Wine Bar, The
MacArthur Park
Mama's
Masa's
Narsai's Cafe
New Joe's
Original Joe's
Orsi
Palm, The
Pierre at Meridien
Pier 23 Cafe
Post Street Bar/Cafe
Restaurant 101
Rotunda, The
Samantha's
Sam's Grill/Seafood
Schroeder's
Scott's Seafood Grill
Sears Fine Foods
Shadows, The
Square One
Squid's Cafe
Sutter 500
Tadich Grill
Trader Vic's
Tu Lan Restaurant

Upstart Crow & Co.
Victor's
Yamato Sukiyaki
Zuni Cafe

East Bay

A la Carte
Augusta's
Bay Wolf Cafe
Benihana
Bridge Creek Cafe
Broadway Terrace Cafe
Cafe at Chez Panisse
Cafe Bistro Oyster Bar
Cafe Fanny
Caffe Venezia
Chez Panisse
China Pavilion
China Station
Dakota Grill & Bar
Edokko
Fat Apple's
Fourth Street Grill
Gertie's Chesapeake Bay
Gulf Coast
India Place
Juan's Place
Lalime's
La Mediterranee
La Mexicana
Le Marquis
Le Metropole
Long Life Vegie House
Mama's Royal Cafe
Mesa
Mikado
Nadine
Norman's
Omnivore
Pavilion Room
Plearn Thai Cuisine
Riera's
Santa Fe Bar & Grill
Scott's Seafood Grill
Siam Cuisine
Spenger's Fish Grotto
Taiwan Restaurant
Via Veneto
Warszawa
Yoshi's

Japantown

Benihana
Ino Sushi

Isobune Sushi
Korea House
Mifune
Sanppo
Seoul Garden

Mission

Bruno's
Cuba
Diamond Street
El Tazumal
La Rondalla
La Taqueria
La Traviata
Le Domino
Nicaragua Restaurant
Taqueria Mission
Taqueria Tepatitlan

Nob Hill

Alexis
Fournou's Ovens
French Room, The
Le Club
L'Etoile
Nob Hill Cafe
Nob Hill Restaurant
Squire Restaurant
Vanessi's

North Beach

Alfred's
Amelio's
Basta Pasta
Beethoven
Buca Giovanni
Caffe Roma
Caffe Sport
Dixie Cafe
Fior d'Italia
Little Joe's
Mamma's
New San Remo
North Beach
Raf
Ristorante Grifone
Tommaso's
Trattoria Contadina
U.S. Restaurant
Vanessi's
Washington Sq. Bar/Grill

Pacific Heights

Da Sandro
El Drisco Hotel
Elite Cafe, The
Jackson Fillmore Trattoria
Kim's
La Mediterranee
La Rocca's Oyster Bar
Le Castel
Osome
Pacific Hts. Bar & Grill
Trio Cafe
Vivande Porta Via

Potrero Hill

Aux Delices
San Francisco BBQ
S. Asimakopoulous
Yet Wah

Richmond

Acropolis Deli
Alejandro's Sociedad
Angkor Wat
Bill's Place
Cafe Riggio
Cambodia House
Cheer's Cafe
China House
Chu Lin
Clement St. Bar/Grill
Cliff House
Courtyard, The
Ebisu
El Sombrero
Ernesto's
Golden Turtle
Hahn's Hibachi
Hunan Restaurant
Java Restaurant
Kabuto Sushi
Khan Toke Thai
King of China
Kirin
Le Cyrano
Le St. Tropez
Mai's
Mandalay
Mike's Chinese Cuisine
Milano Pizzeria
Miz Brown's Feed Bag
Napoli
Narai

Ocean
Pacific Cafe
Ton Kiang
Vegi Food
Yet Wah

SOMA

Billboard Cafe
Cadillac Bar/Restaurant
Don Ramon's
Hamburger Mary's
Little Joe's
Max's Diner
Rings
Umberto's

Sunset

Little Joe's
Mai's
Mamounia
Tien Fu

Union Street

Balboa Cafe
Brazen Head
Doidge's Kitchen
La Pergola
L'Entrecote de Paris
L'Escargot
Mai's
Monroe's
North India
Parma
Perry's
Pietro's
Pixley Cafe
Prego Ristorante
Restaurant Rodin
Ronayne's
Scott's Seafood Grill
Sugar's Grill/Sushi Bar
Vlasta's
Yoshida-Ya

Van Ness/Polk

Adriatic
Cafe Majestic
Cordon Bleu Vietnamese
Golden Turtle
Hahn's Hibachi
Harris' Restaurant
Mekong
Nikko Sushi

Pasha
Peacock, The
Phnom Penh
Rosalie's
Swan Oyster Depot
Zola's

Wharf

A. Sabella's
Chez Michel
China House
El Tapatio

Gaylord
Green's
Mandarin, The
Maxwell's Plum
Modesto Lanzone's
Old Swiss House
Paprika's Fono
Scoma's
Tokyo Sukiyaki
Vicolo Pizzeria
Waterfront
Yet Wah

BEYOND SAN FRANCISCO

Marin

Adriana's
Alta Mira Hotel
Baci
Barnaby's
Butler's
Cafe Tango
California Cafe
Cantina, The
Caprice, The
Carlo's Italian
Casa Madrona
Christophe
Daniel's
Dock, The
Feng Nian
Flynn's Landing
Giramonti
Goro's Robato
Gray Whale
Guaymas
Guernica
Horizons
India Place
La Ginestra
La Mediterranee
La Petite Auberge
Lark Creek Inn, The
Las Camelias
Le Camembert
Lucca Ristorante
Mandarin House
Marin Joe's
Maurice et Charles
Milly's
Olema Inn, The
Ondine

Ramona
Ristorante Fabrizio
Sam's Anchor Cafe
Samurai
Sand Dollar
Savannah Grill
Scoma's
Yet Wah

Mendocino

Cafe Beaujolais

Monterey

Abalonetti
Fresh Cream
Giuliano's
Rio Grill
Sardine Factory

Napa

Auberge du Soleil
California Cafe
Domaine Chandon
French Laundry
Knickerbockers
Le Rhone
Meadowood
Miramonte
Mustard's Grill
Rose et Lafavour's

Peninsula

Barbarossa
Bella Vista
Benihana
Brothers Deli
Chantilly

Dal Baffo
Gervais
L'Auberge
Le Papillon
L'Escale
MacArthur Park
Mama's
Paolo's
Scott's Seafood Grill
Stanford Park Hotel

Trader Vic's
Yet Wah

Sonoma

Au Relais
California Cafe
John Ash & Co.
Madrona Manor
Sharl's
Station House Cafe

SPECIAL FEATURES AND APPEALS

Bar Scenes

Balboa Cafe
Bentley's
Big Four
Cadillac Bar
Carnelian Room
Chez Michel
Clement St. Bar/Grill
Courtyard, The
Elite Cafe, The
Fior d'Italia
Flynn's Landing
Fog City Diner
Harry's Bar & Grill
Le Central
L'Etoile
London Wine Bar, The
MacArthur Park
Maxwell's Plum
North Beach Restaurant
Pacific Hts. Bar/Grill
Palm
Pat O'Shea's*
Perry's
Prego
Rosalie's
Sam's
Santa Fe Bar & Grill
Sardine Factory
Scott's
Star's
Trader Vic's
Vanessi's
Washington Sq. Bar/Grill

Breakfast

(All major hotels and
the following)
Bridge Creek Cafe
Cafe Bedford
Cafe Fanny
Cafe Majestic
Campton Place
Dakota Grill & Bar
Faz Restaurant & Bar
Gray Whale
King of China
Kuleto's
MacArthur Park
Mama's
Mama's Royal Cafe
Miz Brown's Feed Bag

Pier 23 Cafe
Sears Fine Foods
Spuntino
Station House Cafe

Brunch

Alta Mira Hotel
Augusta's
Au Relais
Balboa Cafe
Barnaby's
Billboard Cafe
Brazen Head
Bridge Creek Cafe
Butler's
Cafe Beaujolais
Cafe Fanny
Cafe Majestic
Cafe Tango
Campton Place
Cantina, The
Caprice, The
Carnelian Room
Cheer's Cafe
China Pavilion
Chu Lin
Clement St. Bar/Grill
Courtyard, The
Daniel's
Eichelbaum & Co. Cafe
El Drisco Hotel
Elite Cafe, The
Fat Apple's
Flynn's Landing
French Room, The
Gaylord Indian
Gertie's Chesapeake Bay
Green's
Guaymas
Hamburger Mary's
Horizons
India Place
Ivy's
John Ash & Co.
Korea House
Kuleto's
Lark Creek Inn, The
Le Camembert
L'Entrecote de Paris

(*Not in Survey)

82

Le Piano Zinc
L'Escale
Long Life Vegie House
MacArthur Park
Madrona Manor
Maxwell's Plum
Mesa
Miz Brown's Feed Bag
Mustard's Grill
Narsai's Cafe
New Joe's
Norman's
North India
Olema Inn, The
Ondine
Pacific Hts. Bar & Grill
Pavilion Room
Perry's
Pier 23 Cafe
Pixley Cafe
Rio Grill
Ronayne's
Rosalie's
Sam's Anchor Cafe
Sand Dollar
Santa Fe Bar & Grill
Savannah Grill
Scott's Seafood Grill
Sears Fine Foods
Sharl's
Tung Fong
Victor's
Washington Sq. Bar/Grill
Waterfront
Zuni Cafe

Business Meetings

Adriatic
Auberge du Soleil
Barnaby's
Benihana
Bruno's
Cafe Beaujolais
Cafe Bedford
Cafe Majestic
Cafe Tango
Caffe Quadro
Caffe Roma
California Cafe
Calif. Culinary Academy
Campton Place
Caprice, The
Caravansary

Carnelian Room
Casa Madrona
Celadon, The
Chambord
Chantilly
Dal Baffo
Da Sandro
Dixie Cafe
Dock, The
Donatello
Don Ramon's
Ebisu
Empress of China
Faz Restaurant & Bar
Feng Nian
Four Star Restaurant
Gertie's Chesapeake Bay
Gervais
Hunan Restaurant
India Place
Iron Horse, The
Jack's
John Ash & Co.
Julius' Castle
Kansai
Korea House
Korean Palace
La Fuente
La Mediterranee
La Mere Duquesne
La Rondalla
Las Mananitas
L'Auberge
Le Camembert
Le Marquis
L'Entrecote de Paris
Le Papillon
Le Rhone
Little Italy
L'Olivier
MacArthur Park
Madrona Manor
Mai's
Mamounia
Mandarin House
Maxwell's Plum
Mesa
Milly's
Miramonte
New Joe's
New San Remo
Nikko Sushi
Nob Hill Restaurant

North Beach
North India
Old Swiss House
Olema Inn, The
Orsi
Osome
Pacific Hts. Bar & Grill
Palm, The
Paolo's
Pasha
Pavilion Room
Peacock, The
Pierre at Meridien
Restaurant 101
Rings
Ristorante Fabrizio
Rosalie's
Rotunda, The
Samantha's
Sardine Factory
Schroeder's
Scott's Seafood Grill
Seoul Garden
Shadows, The
Sharl's
Spenger's Fish Grotto
Squid's Cafe
Stars
Ton Kiang
Trader Vic's
Trattoria Contadina
Umberto's
Vanessi's
Via Veneto
Victor's
Yamato Sukiyaki
Yoshi's
Zola's

Caters

Acropolis Deli
Alta Mira Hotel
Auberge du Soleil
Beethoven
Brad Forrest
Brothers Deli
Cafe Bedford
Cafe d'Arts
Cafe Tango
Caffe Venezia
California Cafe
Cantina, The
Caravansary

Casa Madrona
Celadon, The
Chambord
Chantilly
China Pavilion
Chu Lin
Diamond Street
Dock, The
Donatello
Ebisu
Eichelbaum & Co. Cafe
Faz Restaurant & Bar
Fournou's Ovens
Four Star Restaurant
French Room, The
Gaylord
Gertie's Chesapeake Bay
Goro's Robato
Guernica
Harbor Village
Harry's Bar & Grill
Hunan Restaurant
Hunan Village
India Place
Iron Horse, The
Isobune Sushi
Ivy's
Jackson Fillmore Trattoria
John Ash & Co.
Juan's Place
Kansai
Kim's
King of China
Kinokawa
Knickerbockers
Korean Palace
La Fuente
La Ginestra
Lalime's
La Mediterranee
Las Camelias
Le Camembert
Le Marquis
L'Entrecote de Paris
MacArthur Park
Mamounia
Marin Joe's
Maxwell's Plum
Mesa
Mikado
Mike's Chinese Cuisine
Milly's
Nikko Sushi

Ocean City
Osome
Paolo's
Pasha
Pavilion Room
Pier 23 Cafe
Ramona
Rings
Rotunda, The
San Francisco BBQ
Schroeder's
Seoul Garden
Spuntino
Sugar's Grill/Sushi Bar
Trader Vic's
Vicolo Pizzeria
Vivande Porta Via
Warszawa
Yamato Sukiyaki
Yoshi's
Zola's

Dancing

(Check days and times)
Avenue Ballroom*
  (swing)
Buzzby's* (disco)
Carousel* (ballroom)
Cesar's Latin Palace*
  (Latin)
Copa Club* (soul/salsa)
Fairmont Hotel*
  New Orleans Room
  (Dixieland)
  Tonga (ballroom)
  Venetian Room
  (night club)
Henry's Dance Club*
  (ballroom)
Holiday Inn* (disco)
Hyatt Regency*
  Atrium Lobby (variety
I-Beam* (rock)
Le Club Touche*
  (ballroom)
Oasis* (rock)
Palladium* (rock)
Regent Cafe* (disco)
Rockin' Robin's*
  (jukebox)
St. Francis Hotel*
  Compass Rose
  (ballroom)
  Oz (pop, disco)

Stone, The* (rock)
Trocadero Transfer*
  (disco)

Delivers

(Among the many)
Brothers Deli
Cafe d'Arts
Cambodia House
Eichelbaum & Co. Cafe
Faz Restaurant & Bar
Hunan Village
Knickerbockers
La Fuente
La Mediterranee
Pasha
Vivande Porta Via
Yoshi's

Dessert (D) and Ice Cream (I)

Bud's Ice Cream* (I)
Double Rainbow* (I)
Fono's* (I)
Just Desserts* (D)
Gelato Classico* (I)
Joe's Ice Cream* (I)
Mary's* (D)
Old Uncle Gaylord's* (I)
Rory's Twisted Scoop* (I)
SF Desserts* (D)
Sweet Inspiration* (D)
Swensens* (I)
Toy Boat Dessert Cafe* (D)
True Confections* (D)
Vivoli's* (I)

Dining Alone

Benihana
Bentley's
Bill's Place
China Moon Cafe
Doidge's Kitchen
Elite Cafe
Flynn's Landing
Hamburger Mary's
Hog Heaven
Isobune
Kabuto Sushi
Kinokawa
La Taqueria

(*Not in Survey)

MacArthur Park
Max's Diner
Max's Opera Cafe
Miz Brown's Feed Bag
Nikko
Pacific Hts. Bar & Grill
Perry's
Sam's Anchor Cafe
Schroeder's
Spuntino
Stars
Sushi-gen
Swan Oyster Depot
Tadich Grill

Entertainment

(Check days and times;
complete listing in Sunday
newspapers)
Bentley's (piano)
Cafe Majestic (cabaret)
City Cabaret* (variety)
Christophe's (jazz)
Curtain Call* (piano)
French Room, The
    (piano)
Gold Dust Lounge*
    (Dixieland)
Harris' (piano)
Harry's Bar (piano)
Kimball's* (jazz)
La Fuente
    (music, dancers)
Le Piano Zinc
    (piano, singer)
L'Etoile (piano)
Stars (piano)
Venetian Room*
    (night club)
Washington Sq. Bar/Grill
    (jazz)

Fireplaces

A la Carte
Alta Mira Hotel
Auberge du Soleil
Barbarossa
Bella Vista
Cafe Beaujolais
Cafe Bistro Oyster Bar
Cafe Mozart
Caprice, The
Casa Madrona

Chantilly
Clement St. Bar/Grill
Dock, The
El Tapatio
Fresh Cream
Guaymas
Horizons
Julius' Castle
Knickerbockers
La Fuente
Le Camembert
Le Metropole
Le St. Tropez
Lucca Ristorante
MacArthur Park
Madrona Manor
Miramonte
Neon Chicken
Nikko Sushi
Old Swiss House
Pierre at Meridien
Post St. Bar/Cafe
Rings
Rio Grill
Sand Dollar
Sardine Factory
Sharl's
Warszawa

Game in Season

Amelio's
Auberge du Soleil
Dixie Cafe
Donatello
Eichelbaum & Co. Cafe
El Drisco Hotel
Faz Restaurant & Bar
Fresh Cream
Golden Phoenix
Guaymas
Harry's Bar & Grill
Hayes Street Grill
Ivy's
Jack's
John Ash & Co.
L'Auberge
La Ginestera
Le Castel
Le Papillon
Le Piano Zinc
L'Etoile

(*Not in Survey)

Madrona Manor
Mamounia
Masa's
Maurice et Charles
Mesa
Mustard's Grill
Nob Hill Restaurant
Ondine
Pierre at Meridien
Prego Ristorante
Rings
Rodin
Rosalie
Rose et Lafavour's
Santa Fe Bar & Grill
Sharl's
Squire Restaurant
Stars
Sugar's Grill/Sushi Bar
Sutter 500
Umberto's
Victor's
Vlasta's
Washington Sq. Bar/Grill
Zola's

Garden Dining

Alta Mira Hotel
Auberge du Soleil
Augusta's
Au Relais
Bay Wolf Cafe
Cafe Beaujolais
Caffe Roma
Cambodia House
Cantina, The
Carlo's Italian
Casa Madrona
Chantilly
Cheer's Cafe
Da Sandro
Domaine Chandon
Gertie's Chesapeake Bay
Guaymas
Julius' Castle
Knickerbockers
Lark Creek Inn, The
MacArthur Park
Miramonte
Mustard's Grill
Nikko Sushi
Olema Inn, The
Perry's

Pier 23 Cafe
Riera's
Rings
Santa Fe Bar & Grill
Sardine Factory
Shadows, The
Sharl's
Warszawa
Yamato Sukiyaki

Health/Spa Menus

Balboa Cafe
California Cafe
Ciao Ristorante
Diamond Street
Eichelbaum & Co. Cafe
Fog City Diner
Fourth Street Grill
Green's
Long Life Vegie House
Millie's
Mustard's Grill
Pacific Hts. Bar & Grill
Prego
Rio Grill
Rotunda, The
Santa Fe Bar & Grill
Sonoma Mission Inn*
Tadich Grill
Vegi Food

Hotel Dining

Alta Mira Hotel
Auberge du Soleil
   (Auberge du Soleil)
Bentley's (Galleria Park)
Big Four
   (Huntington Hotel)
Cafe Bedford
   (Bedford Hotel)
Cafe Majestic
   (Majestic Hotel)
Campton Place
   (Campton Place)
Dakota Grill & Bar
   (Shattuck Hotel)
Donatello
   (Donatello Hotel)
El Drisco Hotel
Equinox*
   (Hyatt Regency)

(*Not in Survey)

Fournou's Ovens
  (Stanford Court)
French Room, The
  (Clift Hotel)
Garden Court*
  (Sheraton Palace)
Kuleto's
  (Villa Florence)
L'Etoile
  (Huntington Hotel)
Madrona Manor
  (Madrona Manor)
Masa's (Vintage Court)
Meadowood
  (Meadowood)
Nob Hill Restaurant
  (Mark Hopkins)
One Up*
  (Hyatt Union Sq.)
Palm, The
  (Juliana Hotel)
Pavilion Room
  (Claremont Hotel)
Pierre at Meridien
  (Meridien)
Squire, The
  (Fairmont Hotel)
Stanford Park Hotel
Victor's
  (St. Francis Hotel)

"In" Places

Amelio's
Auberge du Soleil
Balboa Cafe
Barnaby's
Bay Wolf Cafe
Bentley's
Billboard Cafe
Brad Forrest
Bridge Creek Cafe
Broadway Terrace Cafe
Butler's
Cadillac Bar
Cafe at Chez Panisse
Cafe d'Arts
Cafe Riggio
Caffe Sport
Cambodia House
Campton Place
Chez Panisse
China Moon Cafe
Ciao Ristorante

Circolo
Dixie Cafe
Donatello
Doros
Elite Cafe, The
Fat Apple's
Fleur de Lys
Fog City Diner
Fourth Street Grill
French Room, The
Fresh Cream
Gertie's Chesapeake Bay
Green's
Guaymas
Hamburger Mary's
Harbor Village
Hard Rock Cafe
Harris' Restaurant
Harry's Bar & Grill
Hayes Street Grill
John Ash & Co.
Knickerbockers
Lalime's
Le Central
Le Club
L'Etoile
MacArthur Park
Masa's
Max's Diner
Modesto Lanzone's
Mustard's Grill
Pacific Cafe
Pacific Hts. Bar & Grill
Perry's
Pierre at Meridien
Pier 23 Cafe
Plearn Thai Cuisine
Prego Ristorante
Raf
Rings
Rio Grill
Rosalie's
Spuntino
Squid's Cafe
Stars
Sutter 500
Swan Oyster Depot
Tadich Grill
Tommaso's
Washington Sq. Bar/Grill
Zuni Cafe

(*Not in Survey)

Late Late/After Midnight

(All hours are AM; check weekday times which may be earlier)

Alejandro's Sociedad (12)
Balboa Cafe (12)
Basta Pasta (1:30)
Brazen Head (12:45)
Bruno's (2)
Cadillac Bar (12)
Caffe Roma (1)
Ciao (12)
Fog City Diner (12)
Hamburger Mary's (1:30)
Hard Rock Cafe (12)
Harry's Bar & Grill (12)
Imperial Palace (2)
Kabuto Sushi (2)
Korea House (3)
La Rondalla (3:30)
Le Piano Zinc (12)
Mama's (3:30)
Marin Joe's (12:45)
Max's Diner (1)
Max's Opera Cafe (1)
Original Joe's (1:30)
Pasha (12)
Siam Cuisine (12)
Taiwan (2)
Tien Fu (2:30)
Trader Vic's (12:30)
Yoshi's (12)
Yuet Lee (3)

Music

(Check days and times, and newspapers for exact information)

Bajones* (Latin)
Baybrick Inn* (rock)
Buzzby's* (rock)
Cesar's Latin Palace* (Latin)
Chi Chi Club* (rock)
Full Moon Saloon* (rock)
Gold Dust Lounge* (jazz)
Great American Music Hall* (various)
Greek Taverna* (jazz)
I-Beam* (rock)
Jazz Workshop* (jazz)
Last Day Saloon* (rock)
Pasand Lounge* (jazz)
Roland's* (Latin)
Saloon, The* (rock)
Stone, The* (rock)

Noteworthy Newcomers

Alessia†
Angkor Wat
Bentley's
Billboard Cafe
Brad Forrest
Broadway Terrace Cafe
Butler's
Cafe Fanny
Cafe Majestic
Cafe Tango
Caffe Quadro
China Moon Cafe
Circolo
Dakota Grill & Bar
Dixie Cafe
Faz Restaurant & Bar
Fog City Diner
Gertie's Chesapeake Bay
Guaymas
Harbor Village
Harry's Bar & Grill
Jil's Trianon
Kenwood Restaurant/Bar†
Kim's
Knickerbockers
Kuleto's
Lalime's
Max's Diner
Raf
Restaurant 101
Rings
Samantha's
Savannah Grill
Silks†
Spuntino

Offbeat

Acropolis Deli
Bentley's
Billboard Cafe
Brad Forrest
Bridge Creek Cafe
Brothers Deli
Cadillac Bar

(*Not in Survey)
(†Good prospects opening as we go to press)

Cafe at Chez Panisse
Cafe d'Arts
Cafe Tango
Caffe Sport
Calif. Culinary Academy
Ciao Ristorante
Fat Apple's
Fog City Diner
Gertie's Chesapeake Bay
Green's
Hambuger Mary's
Hard Rock Cafe
La Rondalla
Max's Diner
Max's Opera Cafe
Pasha
Pier 23 Cafe
Plearn Thai Cuisine
Raf
Rosalie's
S. Asimakopoulous
Seoul Garden
Squid's Cafe
Washington Sq. Bar/Grill
Yoshi's

Outdoor Dining

Alta Mira Hotel
Auberge du Soleil
Augusta's
Au Relais
Baci
Barnaby's
Bay Wolf Cafe
Broadway Terrace Cafe
Cafe at Chez Panisse
Caffe Quadro
Caffe Roma
California Cafe
Cantina, The
Cheer's Cafe
Da Sandro
Dock, The
Domaine Chandon
Gertie's Chesapeake Bay
Gray Whale
Guaymas
Horizons
Knickerbockers
La Fuente
Las Camelias
Las Mananitas
Le Rhone

L'Escale
MacArthur Park
Madrona Manor
Mesa
Miramonte
Olema Inn, The
Paprika's Fono
Perry's
Pier 23 Cafe
Restaurant 101
Rings
Samantha's
Sam's Anchor Cafe
Sand Dollar
Sharl's
Vicolo Pizzeria

Parking Difficult

Alejandro's Sociedad
A. Sabella's
Asia Garden
Beethoven
Bentley's
Brazen Head
Bridge Creek Cafe
Buca Giovanni
Cafe at Chez Panisse
Cafe Beaujolais
Cafe Bedford
Cafe Bistro Oyster Bar
Cafe Mozart
Cafe Riggio
Caffe Quadro
Caffe Roma
Caffe Sport
Caravansary
Celadon, The
Chambord
Cheer's Cafe
Chez Michel
Chez Panisse
China Moon Cafe
Clement St. Bar/Grill
Cuba
Da Sandro
Diamond Street
Dixie Cafe
Dock, The
Doidge's Kitchen
Elite Cafe, The
El Sombrero
Empress of China
Ernesto's

Faz Restaurant & Bar
Fior d'Italia
Flynn's Landing
Fog City Diner
Fournou's Ovens
Four Star
Gaylord
Golden Phoenix
Guaymas
Hahn's Hibachi
Hunan Restaurant
Hunan Village
Imperial Palace
India House
Iron Horse, The
Jack's
Jackson Fillmore Trattoria
Jil's Trianon
Kan's
Kansai
Kinokawa
La Fuente
La Mediterranee
La Mexicana
La Pergola Ristorante
La Taqueria
Le Candide
Le Central
L'Olivier
MacArthur Park
Mai's
Mama's
Mama's Royal Cafe
Mandarin, The
Masa's
Maxwell's Plum
Milano Pizzeria
Modesto Lanzone's
Narai
Narsai's Cafe
New Joe's
Nob Hill Cafe
Nob Hill Restaurant
Old Swiss House
Original Joe's
Orsi
Osome
Palm, The
Paprika's Fono
Perry's
Pier 23 Cafe
Pietro's
Pixley Cafe

Plearn Thai Cuisine
Post St. Bar/Cafe
Prego Ristorante
Rotunda, The
Samantha's
Sam's Grill
Schroeder's
Sears Fine Foods
South China Cafe
Spuntino
Sugar's Grill/Sushi Bar
Sushi Gen
Sutter 500
Tadich Grill
Taqueria Tepatitlan
Tokyo Sukiyaki
Tommaso's
Ton Kiang
Trattoria Contadina
Tung Fong
U.S. Restaurant
Vanessi's
Vicolo Pizzeria
Washington Sq. Bar/Grill
Yamato Sukiyaki
Yet Wah
Yoshida-Ya
Yuet Lee

Parties
(see also Private Rooms)
Auberge du Soleil
Balboa Cafe
Big Four
Carnelian Room
Casa Madrona
Ciao Ristorante
Clement Street Bar/Grill
Courtyard, The
Flynn's Landing
French Room, The
Fournou's Ovens
Giramonti
Guaymas
Harris' Restaurant
John Ash & Co.
La Traviata
Maxwell's Plum
Mustard's Grill
Prego
Rings
Santa Fe Bar & Grill
Square One

Station House Cafe
Stars
Trader Vic's

People-Watching

Balboa Cafe
Cadillac Bar
Elite Cafe, The
Fog City Diner
Harry's Bar & Grill
Le Central
Le Piano Zinc
L'Etoile
London Wine Bar, The
MacArthur Park
Pacific Hts. Bar & Grill
Perry's
Raf
Stars
Trader Vic's
Washington Sq. Bar/Grill
Zuni Cafe

Power Scenes

Campton Place
Doros
French Room, The
Le Central
L'Etoile
Sam's Grill
Sardine Factory
Stars
Tadich Grill
Trader Vic's
Vanessi's
Washington Sq. Bar/Grill

Private Rooms

Abalonetti
A la Carte
Alejandro's Sociedad
Alexis
Alfred's
Alta Mira Hotel
A. Sabella's
Auberge du Soleil
Au Relais
Barbarossa
Bruno's
Cafe Bedford
Cafe Majestic
Cafe Mozart
Cafe Tango

California Cafe
Calif. Culinary Academy
Cambodia House
Campton Place
Caprice, The
Carnelian Room
Casa Madrona
Celadon, The
Chambord
Chantilly
Chez Michel
China House
China Pavilion
Chu Lin
Ciao Ristorante
Dal Baffo
Dixie Cafe
Dock, The
Donatello
Don Ramon's
Ebisu
El Drisco Hotel
Empress of China
Ernie's
Faz Restaurant & Bar
Fior d'Italia
Fournou's Ovens
French Room, The
Gaylord
Gervais
Guaymas
Guernica
Harris' Restaurant
Harry's Bar & Grill
Hunan Restaurant
Imperial Palace
India Place
Iron Horse, The
Jil's Trianon
Jack's
John Ash & Co.
Julius' Castle
Kabuto Sushi
Kansai
Khan Toke Thai
Korea House
Korean Palace
La Fuente
Lalime's
La Mere Duquesne
Lark Creek Inn, The
Las Mananitas
L'Auberge

Le Camembert
Le Metropole
L'Entrecote de Paris
Le Papillon
Little Italy
L'Olivier
Lucca Ristorante
MacArthur Park
Madrona Manor
Mai's
Mamounia
Mandarin House
Marin Joe's
Maxwell's Plum
Mesa
Miramonte
Modesto Lanzone's
Nadine
New Joe's
New San Remo
Nikko Sushi
Nob Hill Restaurant
North Beach
North India
Ocean
Old Swiss House
Olema Inn, The
Orsi
Palm, The
Paolo's
Paprika's Fono
Pasha
Pierre at Meridien
Restaurant 101
Rings
Samantha's
Sam's Grill
Samurai
Sardine Factory
Schroeder's
Seoul Garden
Shadows, The
Sharl's
Spenger's Fish Grotto
Square One
Squid's Cafe
Sushi Gen
Tokyo Sukiyaki
Trader Vic's
Trattoria Contadina
Umberto's
Vanessi's
Via Veneto

Vlasta's
Yamato Sukiyaki
Yet Wah
Yoshida-Ya
Yoshi's

Prix Fixe Menus

Abalonetti
Adriana's
Alexis
Alta Mira Hotel
Auberge du Soleil
Au Relais
Barbarossa
Cafe at Chez Panisse
Cafe Bedford
Cafe Mozart
Cafe Tango
Calif. Culinary Academy
Carnelian Room
Celadon, The
Chez Panisse
Circolo
Diamond Street
Donatello
Ebisu
Hunan Restaurant
India House
Jack's
Korean Palace
Lalime's
Las Mananitas
Le Papillon
Le Piano Zinc
Le Rhone
Madrona Manor
Mamounia
Masa's
Maurice et Charles
Miramonte
New San Remo
Nob Hill Cafe
North Beach
North India
Palm, The
Pasha
Pierre at Meridien
Restaurant 101
Restaurant Rodin
Samurai
San Francisco BBQ
Schroeder's
Scott's Seafood Grill

Seoul Garden
Shadows, The
Sharl's
Squire Restaurant
Umberto's
Vanessi's
Victor's
Yamato Sukiyaki

Pubs

Harry's Bar*
Liverpool Lil's*
London Wine Bar, The
Patty O'Shea's*
Perry's

Reservations Essential

Adriana's
Alejandro's Sociedad
Alfred's
Amelio's
Angkor Wat
Auberge du Soleil
Baci
Barbarossa
Bentley's
Butler's
Cafe Beaujolais
Cafe Bedford
Cafe d'Arts
Cafe Majestic
Cafe Mozart
Calif. Culinary Academy
Campton Place
Chambord
Cheer's Cafe
Chez Michel
Chez Panisse
Circolo
Courtyard, The
Dakota Grill & Bar
Domaine Chandon
Donatello
Doros
Edokko
Ernie's
Faz Restaurant & Bar
Fleur de Lys
Fournou's Ovens
Fourth Street Grill
French Room, The
Fresh Cream
Giramonti

Giuliano's
Green's
Guaymas
Harris' Restaurant
Harry's Bar & Grill
Hayes Street Grill
Ironwood Cafe
Jack's
Jil's Trianon
John Ash & Co.
Kuleto's
Lalime's
Lark Creek Inn, The
Le Castel
Le Central
Le Club
Le Piano Zinc
Le Rhone
L'Etoile
MacArthur Park
Madrona Manor
Mandarin, The
Masa's
Maurice et Charles
Miramonte
Mustard's Grill
Nob Hill Cafe
Nob Hill Restaurant
North India
Olema Inn, The
Pacific Hts. Bar & Grill
Palm, The
Phnom Penh
Pierre at Meridien
Raf
Restaurant 101
Rio Grill
Rosalie's
Rose et Lafavour's
Square One
Squire Restaurant
Stars
Sutter 500
Trader Vic's
Washington Sq. Bar/Grill
Zuni Cafe

Romantic Spots

Alexis
Alta Mira Hotel
Amelio's

(*Not in Survey)

Auberge du Soleil
Barbarossa
Barnaby's
Bay Wolf Cafe
Bella Vista
Brazen Head
Cafe d'Arts
Cafe Mozart
Campton Place
Caprice, The
Carnelian Room
Casa Madrona
Chez Michel
Chez Panisse
Christophe
Circolo
Domaine Chandon
Donatello
Doros
El Drisco Hotel
Fleur de Lys
Fournou's Ovens
French Room, The
Gaylord
Gertie's Chesapeake Bay
Harris' Restaurant
Harry's Bar & Grill
India House
Julius' Castle
Kim's
L'Auberge
Le Castel
Le Club
L'Etoile
Madrona Manor
Masa's
Maurice et Charles
Miramonte
Modesto Lanzone's
Paolo's
Pierre at Meridien
Pier 23 Cafe
Plearn Thai Cuisine
Prego Ristorante
Raf
Rosalie's
Squire Restaurant
Victor's
Waterfront

Singles Scenes
Balboa Cafe
Cadillac Bar

Cafe Riggio
Ciao Ristorante
Elite Cafe, The
London Wine Bar, The
Harry's Bar & Grill
Harry's Bar*
MacArthur Park
Pacific Hts. Bar & Grill
Perry's
Sam's Anchor Cafe
Stars

Takeout
Acropolis Deli
Asia Garden
Aux Delices
Baci
Brazen Head
Brothers Deli
Cadillac Bar
Cafe Beaujolais
Cafe d'Arts
Cafe Tango
Caffe Roma
Caffe Venezia
California Cafe
Calif. Culinary Academy
Cambodia House
Campton Place
Cantina, The
Caravansary
Casa Madrona
Celadon, The
Cheer's Cafe
China House
China Pavilion
Christophe
Chu Lin
Ciao Ristorante
Clement St. Bar/Grill
Cordon Bleu Vietnamese
Daniel's
Dock, The
Doidge's Kitchen
Don Ramon's
Ebisu
Eichelbaum & Co. Cafe
El Sombrero
El Tapatio
El Tazumal
Ernesto's

(*Not in Survey)

Fat Apple's
Feng Nian
Flynn's Landing
Gertie's Chesapeake Bay
Goro's Robato
Gray Whale
Green's
Harbor Village
Hunan Restaurant
Imperial Palace
India Place
Ino Sushi
Isobune Sushi
Java
Juan's Place
Kabuto Sushi
Kim's
King of China
Kinokawa
Kirin
Knickerbockers
Korea House
Korean Palace
La Fuente
La Ginestra
La Mediterranee
La Mexicana
La Rocca's Oyster Bar
La Rondalla
La Taqueria
L'Escale
Little Italy
Little Joe's
Long Life Vegie House
MacArthur Park
Mai's
Mandarin House
Mandarin, The
Max's Diner
Max's Opera Cafe
Mekong
Mifune
Mikado
Mike's Chinese Cuisine
Miz Brown's Feed Bag
Narai
Narsai's Cafe
New Joe's
Nicaragua
Nikko Sushi
North Beach
North India

Ocean
Ocean City
Original Joe's
Osome
Pasha
Peacock, The
Pier 23 Cafe
Plearn Thai Cuisine
Ramona
Rings
Rotunda, The
Samurai
San Francisco BBQ
Seoul Garden
Siam Cuisine
South China Cafe
Spenger's Fish Grotto
Spuntino
Squid's Cafe
Sugar's Grill/Sushi Bar
Sushi Gen
Sutter 500
Swan Oyster Depot
Taiwan Restaurant
Taqueria Tepatitlan
Tien Fu
Ton Kiang
Trattoria Contadina
Trio Cafe
Tu Lan
Tung Fong
Vegi Food
Via Veneto
Vicolo Pizzeria
Vivande Porta Via
Warszawa
Yamato Sukiyaki
Yet Wah
Yoshida-Ya
Yuet Lee

Teas
(Check times and prices)
Campton Place*
Donatello*
Fairmont (Cirque Room)*
Four Seasons Clift Hotel*
Mark Hopkins Hotel*
Stanford Court Hotel*
St. Francis Hotel*

(*Not in Survey)

Teenagers and Other Youthful Spirits

Basta Pasta
Benihana
Billboard Cafe
Cadillac Bar
Dixie Cafe
Elite Cafe, The
El Tapatio
Ernesto's
Fat Apples
Flynn's Landing
Fog City Diner
Grey Whale
Guaymas
Hamburger Mary's
Hard Rock Cafe
Hog Heaven
Isobune
Kabuto Sushi
MacArthur Park
Maxwell's Plum
Neon Chicken
New Joe's
Perry's
Prego
Rings
Rosalie
Sam's Anchor Cafe
Tomasso's
Trader Vic's
Waterfront

Valet Parking

Alexis
Alfred's
Alta Mira Hotel
Amelio's
Auberge du Soleil
Basta Pasta
Cafe Majestic
California Cafe
Calif. Culinary Academy
Campton Place
Caprice, The
Casa Madrona
China House
Ciao Ristorante
Donatello
Doros
Ernie's
Fleur de Lys
French Room, The

Hard Rock Cafe
Harris' Restaurant
Harry's Bar & Grill
Horizons
John Ash & Co.
Julius' Castle
Korea House
Las Mananitas
Le Castel
Le Club
L'Entrecote de Paris
Le St. Tropez
L'Etoile
New San Remo
Nikko Sushi
North Beach
Ondine
Pacific Hts. Bar & Grill
Pasha
Peacock, The
Pierre at Meridien
Raf
Restaurant 101
Restaurant Rodin
Rings
Ristorante Grifone
Rosalie's
Sardine Factory
Scoma's
Scott's Seafood Grill
Shadows, The
Square One
Trader Vic's
Victor's
Vivande Porta Via
Waterfront
Yoshi's

Visitors on Expense Accounts

Alexis
Amelio's
Blue Fox
Butler's
Campton Place
Carnelian Room
Donatello
Doros
Ernie's
Fleur de Lys
Fournou's Ovens
French Room, The
Harris' Restaurant

John Ash & Co.
Le Castel
Le Club
L'Etoile
Masa's
Miramonte
Nob Hill Restaurant
Palm, The
Pierre at Meridien
Squire Restaurant
Stars
Trader Vic's

Wheelchair Access

(Check for
restroom access)
Adolph's
Amelio's
A. Sabella's
Benihana
Bill's Place
Cadillac Bar
Cafe Bedford
Cafe d'Arts
Cafe Riggio
Carnelian Room
Chez Michel
China House
Ciao Ristorante
Da Sandro
Doidge's Kitchen
Donatello's
Doros
Fior d'Italia
Fleur de Lys
Fournou's Ovens
Fourth Street Grill
French Room, The
Harris' Restaurant
Hayes Street Grill
Hippo
Hunan Restaurant
Kirin
MacArthur Park
Mai's
Mama's
Mandalay
Mandarin, The
Max's Opera Cafe
Mustard's Grill
Narai
Nikko
Nob Hill Restaurant

North India
Pacific Hts. Bar & Grill
Palm, The
Pierre at Meridien
Restaurant 101
Schroeder's
Scoma's
Scott's Seafood
Trader Vic's
Vanessi's

Winning Wine Lists

Amelio's
Auberge du Soleil
Balboa Cafe
Barbarossa
Barnaby's
Bay Wolf Cafe
Bentley's
Billboard Cafe
Brad Forrest
Broadway Terrace Cafe
Buca Giovanni
Cafe at Chez Panisse
Cafe Bedford
Cafe Bistro Oyster Bar
Cafe d'Arts
Cafe Fanny
Cafe Majestic
Cafe Mozart
Cafe Tango
Caffe Venezia
California Cafe
Calif. Culinary Academy
Campton Place
Caprice, The
Carnelian Room
Celadon, The
Chantilly
Chez Michel
Chez Panisse
China Moon Cafe
Christophe
Ciao Ristorante
Circolo
Dal Baffo
Dixie Cafe
Domaine Chandon
Donatello
Doros
Eichelbaum & Co. Cafe
El Drisco Hotel
Elite Cafe, The

Ernie's
Fog City Diner
Fournou's Ovens
Fourth Street Grill
French Room, The
Fresh Cream
Green's
Harris' Restaurant
Harry's Bar & Grill
Hayes Street Grill
Iron Horse, The
John Ash & Co.
Julius' Castle
Knickerbockers
Kuleto's
L'Auberge
Le Castel
Le Central
Le Club
L'Etoile
London Wine Bar, The
MacArthur Park
Madrona Manor
Masa's
Maurice et Charles
Miramonte
Modesto Lanzone's
Mustard's Grill
Nob Hill Restaurant
North India
Pacific Hts. Bar & Grill
Paolo's
Pavilion Room
Pier 23 Cafe
Pixley Cafe
Plearn Thai Cuisine
Post Street Bar/Cafe
Prego Ristorante
Raf
Rose et Lafavour's
Santa Fe Bar & Grill
Spuntino
Square One
Squire Restaurant
Stars
Sutter 500
Trader Vic's
Umberto's
Victor's
Vivande Porta Via
Zuni Cafe

Worth a Trip
Auberge du Soleil (Napa)
French Laundry (Napa)
Fresh Cream (Carmel)
John Ash & Co. (Sonoma)
Madrona Manor
    (Sonoma)
Meadowood (Napa)
Miramonte (Napa)
Mount View Hotel*
    (Napa)
Mustard's Grill (Napa)
Rio Grill (Carmel)
Rose et Lafavour's (Napa)
Sonoma Mission Inn*
    (Sonoma)
Station House Cafe
    (Point Reyes)

Young Children
(Besides fast food places)
Abalonetti
Alejandro's Sociedad
Asia Garden
Basta Pasta
Benihana
Bill's Place
Brothers Deli
Cafe Riggio
China Station
Chu Lin
Cliff House
Empress of China
Ernesto's
Fat Apples
Hahn's Hibachi
Hard Rock Cafe
Kan's
King of China
Kirin
La Taqueria
Little Italy
Little Joe's
Marin Joe's
Max's Diner
Mifune
Milano Pizzeria
Miz Brown's Feed Bag
New Joe's
Ocean
Original Joe's

(*Not in Survey)

Sam's Anchor Cafe
Samurai
San Francisco BBQ
Scott's Seafood Grill
Sears Fine Foods
Seoul Garden
Spenger's Fish Grotto

Station House Cafe
Swan Oyster Depot
Tommaso's
Ton Kiang
Trader Vic's
Vicolo Pizzeria
Yet Wah

RATING SHEETS

To aid your participation in next year's Survey

| F | D | S | C |

| | | | $ |
Ratings

Restaurant Name _____
Phone _____
Date Visited _____
Maitre D' _____
Comments _____
_____
_____

| | | | $ |
Ratings

Restaurant Name _____
Phone _____
Date Visited _____
Maitre D' _____
Comments _____
_____
_____

| | | | $ |
Ratings

Restaurant Name _____
Phone _____
Date Visited _____
Maitre D' _____
Comments _____
_____
_____

| | | | $ |
Ratings

Restaurant Name _____
Phone _____
Date Visited _____
Maitre D' _____
Comments _____
_____
_____

| **F** | **D** | **S** | **C** |

| | | | $ |
Ratings

Restaurant Name _____
Phone _____
Date Visited _____
Maitre D' _____
Comments _____
_____
_____

| | | | $ |
Ratings

Restaurant Name _____
Phone _____
Date Visited _____
Maitre D' _____
Comments _____
_____
_____

| | | | $ |
Ratings

Restaurant Name _____
Phone _____
Date Visited _____
Maitre D' _____
Comments _____
_____
_____

| | | | $ |
Ratings

Restaurant Name _____
Phone _____
Date Visited _____
Maitre D' _____
Comments _____
_____
_____

| **F** | **D** | **S** | **C** |

| | | | | $ |
Ratings

Restaurant Name _____
Phone _____
Date Visited _____
Maitre D' _____
Comments _____
_____
_____

| | | | | $ |
Ratings

Restaurant Name _____
Phone _____
Date Visited _____
Maitre D' _____
Comments _____
_____
_____

| | | | | $ |
Ratings

Restaurant Name _____
Phone _____
Date Visited _____
Maitre D' _____
Comments _____
_____
_____

| | | | | $ |
Ratings

Restaurant Name _____
Phone _____
Date Visited _____
Maitre D' _____
Comments _____
_____
_____

| **F** | **D** | **S** | **C** |

| | | | $ |
Ratings

Restaurant Name _____

Phone _____

Date Visited _____

Maitre D' _____

Comments _____

_____

_____

| | | | $ |
Ratings

Restaurant Name _____

Phone _____

Date Visited _____

Maitre D' _____

Comments _____

_____

_____

| | | | $ |
Ratings

Restaurant Name _____

Phone _____

Date Visited _____

Maitre D' _____

Comments _____

_____

_____

| | | | $ |
Ratings

Restaurant Name _____

Phone _____

Date Visited _____

Maitre D' _____

Comments _____

_____

_____

| F | D | S | C |

| | | |$ |
Ratings

Restaurant Name _____
Phone _____
Date Visited _____
Maitre D' _____
Comments _____
_____
_____

| | | |$ |
Ratings

Restaurant Name _____
Phone _____
Date Visited _____
Maitre D' _____
Comments _____
_____
_____

| | | |$ |
Ratings

Restaurant Name _____
Phone _____
Date Visited _____
Maitre D' _____
Comments _____
_____
_____

| | | |$ |
Ratings

Restaurant Name _____
Phone _____
Date Visited _____
Maitre D' _____
Comments _____
_____
_____

WINE VINTAGE CHART 1970-1985

These ratings are designed to help you select wine to go with your meal. They are on the same 0 to 30 scale used throughout this Guide. The ratings reflect both the quality of the vintage year and the wine's readiness to drink. Thus, if a wine is not fully mature or is over the hill, its rating has been reduced. 1971, '72, '73, '74 and '77 vintages have been omitted because these were either poor wine years or are no longer widely available in restaurants.

WHITES	70	75	76	78	79	80	81	82	83	84	85
French:											
Burgundy	–	–	19	25	25	15	23	20	23	19	24
Loire Valley	–	–	–	–	–	12	15	17	18	15	19
Champagne	21	25	19	–	20	–	20	21	20	–	22
Sauternes	26	26	25	12	12	20	20	16	22	9	15
California:											
Chardonnay	–	–	–	–	–	21	19	17	20	19	22

REDS	70	75	76	78	79	80	81	82	83	84	85
French:											
Bordeaux	28	27	20	26	25	15	24	26	24	15	22
Burgundy	17	–	22	28	24	20	16	23	23	17	25
Rhone	22	–	17	26	20	18	16	19	24	15	25
Beaujolais	–	–	–	–	–	–	18	17	24	15	27
California:											
Cabernet Sauvignon	–	–	–	20	21	22	20	19	19	21	20
Zinfandel	–	–	–	–	–	13	13	13	12	15	18
Italian: *											
Brunello	23	16	12	20	19	18	21	23	19	11	18
Chianti	18	14	11	17	14	13	15	17	16	10	19
Piemonte	21	9	12	28	23	14	16	25	17	11	20

*Wines such as **Bardolino** and **Valpolicella** do not pretend to greatness, but enjoy popularity for being reliably good year-in, year-out. They are usually reasonably priced.